YEAR-ROUND
ASSEMBLIES

Thirty theme-based Bible stories for collective and all-age worship
with follow-up activities

BRIAN OGDEN & JO DOBBS

Published by
The Bible Reading Fellowship
First Floor, Elsfield Hall
15–17 Elsfield Way, Oxford OX2 8FG

ISBN 1 84101 328 5
First published 2003
10 9 8 7 6 5 4 3 2 1 0

Acknowledgments
Scripture quotations are taken from the *Contemporary English Version* © American Bible
Society 1991, 1992, 1995. Used by permission/Anglicizations © British and Foreign Bible
Society 1997.

Qualifications and Curriculum Authority copyright material is reproduced under the terms of
HMSO Guidance Note 8.

A catalogue record for this book is available from the British Library

Printed and bound in Malta

FOREWORD

As soon as the assembly finished, I knew this was going to be a really helpful and popular book for everyone involved in taking collective worship in schools. The easy-to-use format and style, delivered through a variety of approaches, is user-friendly and informative. The children thoroughly enjoyed the first interactive assembly we tried about David. Over the following weeks the children, teachers and I really felt we were getting to know this amazing personality from the Old Testament. In the spring and summer terms we felt the same fascination for the lives of Jesus and Peter.

In *Year-round assemblies*, Brian Ogden has created yet another winning formula for delivering collective worship. This excellent assembly book reflects Brian's enthusiasm and love for presenting biblical stories, making them fun, interesting and relevant.

As head teacher of The Michael Syddall CE Aided Primary School, I have been most fortunate to work closely with Jo Dobbs for several years. As an energetic RE coordinator and primary teacher, Jo has always enthused about RE, collective worship and the approach of children to a spiritual threshold. The follow-up activities in this book reflect her practical approach to PSHCE work with children.

David Stott
Headteacher, The Michael Syddall CE Aided Primary School

This book is dedicated with love to
James Charles Dobbs
who, when older, will participate in many assemblies

CONTENTS

SUMMER TERM: PETER

INTRODUCTION

Year-round assemblies offers something a little different from most assembly books. Many offer pick-and-mix assemblies whereby the user can dip into the book and choose from a diversity of themes. *Year-round assemblies* is sequential—each assembly follows on from the one before. The autumn term contains assemblies on the life of David and leads into an introduction to Jesus, so often referred to as 'son of David', through his birth. The spring term follows Jesus' life from childhood to the events of Easter. The summer term concentrates on the adventures of Peter, from the time of his decision to follow Jesus through into the Acts of the Apostles. The whole structure encourages a sense of anticipation and learning development. The final assembly is a celebration of the whole year's content.

Each assembly is accompanied by extension material closely linking the theme of the assembly to Personal Social and Health Education/Citizenship (PSHCE) and the relevant National Curriculum references are given. The suggested extension activities cover a wide variety of objectives and include elements for:

 discussion   writing

 drama   research

Each term consists of ten assemblies. There are three different types of assembly. The first type uses two adult narrators, indicated by the letter A. These assemblies generally come at the beginning and end of a term when there is less time to prepare class-led assemblies. The second is a class-led assembly where one class or group of children is responsible for both the narration and the miming of the story. These assemblies are indicated by the letter B. The third type, indicated by the letter C, usually led by either one or two adult narrators, is interactive. Everyone joins in by making a certain defined response.

Each assembly has a stated theme, aim and Bible reference. Any preparation required is clearly indicated in the sidebar for the assembly. For ease of reference, visual aids are listed at the back of the book.

Hymns are suggested from the BBC's *The Complete Come and Praise* book. In addition there are three new songs, one for each term, which help to summarize the teaching. Music notation is provided for these songs, with simple accompaniments.

★★★ AUTUMN TERM ★★★

INTRODUCTION TO THE AUTUMN TERM

The autumn term starts with a brief introduction to David. You may wish to give more background information to the situation in Israel than is possible to provide here. David's life story forms the content of seven assemblies and is summarized in the eighth. A link is made in the ninth assembly between David and Jesus, which then leads into the Christmas story. As the assemblies follow a natural sequence, it is important to keep to the order suggested.

It is strongly recommended that where two narrators (A and B) are shown, these should be adults.

The 'Good news, bad news' song provides a new verse each week during the autumn term. The verses summarize the content of the assembly.

GOOD NEWS, BAD NEWS

Verse 1
David, shepherd on the hillside,
Caring for his rams and ewes,
Samuel turned up with this
                    message,
'I've got very good news for you!'

> **Chorus**
> *Good news, bad news,*
> *Which do you want first?*
> *Do you want the best?*
> *Or do you want the worst?*

Chorus…

Verse 2
David, visiting his brothers,
Found them in a dreadful stew.
David shouted to Goliath,
'I've got very bad news for you!'

Chorus…

Verse 3
Saul had sudden fits of temper,
No one quite knew what to do.
'David plays relaxing music.
I've got very good news for you!'

Verse 4
Saul got envious of David,
Even tried to kill him too.
Michal saw the soldiers waiting,
'I've got very bad news for you!'

Chorus…

Verse 5
Saul's son was a friend to David.
Jonathan's love for him was true.
Saul and Jonathan killed in battle,
'I've got very bad news for you!'

Chorus…

Reproduced with permission from *Year-round assemblies* published by BRF 2003 (1 84101 328 5)

Verse 6
David, king of Israel's nation,
Jebusites he overthrew.
Jerusalem becomes his city.
'I've got very good news for you!'

Chorus…

Verse 7
David walking on the roof top,
Where Bethsheba is in view.
Kills Uriah, the faithful soldier,
'I've got very bad news for you!'

Chorus…

Verse 8
David, shepherd, king, musician,
From Old Testament to New,
Jesus, son of David, followed.
'I've got very good news for you!'

Chorus…

Verse 9
Brightest lights and flying angels,
Terrified sheep and shepherds
                                    too.
'Don't be scared, I've come
                      from heaven—
I've got very good news for you!'

Chorus…

Verse 10
Mary's baby, born in stable,
To the shepherds now on view.
There in David's town the
                          Saviour.
'I've got very good news for you!'

 Reproduced with permission from *Year-round assemblies* published by BRF 2003 (1 84101 328 5)

Good News, Bad News

Music by Jo Dobbs
Lyrics by Brian Ogden

CHOSEN

Theme

David is chosen as king from an unusual background. We all have worth as individuals and can develop skills to manage our responsibilities.

Aim

To introduce David as the topic of the term's assemblies.

Bible reference

1 SAMUEL 16:1–13

Key verse

1 SAMUEL 16:13

Samuel poured the oil on David's head while his brothers watched. At that moment, the Spirit of the Lord took control of David and stayed with him from then on.

Preparation

- World map showing Israel (on page 16)
- Timeline showing David, birth of Jesus and the year 2000 (on page 17)

NB: Children may be introduced to mime the parts of David (plus a small flock of 'sheep'), Saul and Samuel towards the end of the narration.

★★★★★★★★★★★★★★★★★★★★★★★★★★★★★★★★★★★★★★★

CAST

Two leaders/narrators (A and B)
David
A small flock of sheep
King Saul
Samuel

STORY

A Our assemblies this term will tell the story of one man.

B His name is David. David lived in the country which today we call Israel.

Show the world map and indicate Israel.

A David lived about one thousand years before Jesus was born.

Show and discuss the timeline.

Enter David and small flock of sheep.

B   Sheep. They were everywhere. As far as David could see, the hillside was covered in sheep. Most of them were doing what sheep do best…

A   …eating. David was still only a teenager but he had been looking after the family sheep for almost as long as he could remember. There were busy times at lambing.

B   There were frightening times when a wolf threatened the herd.

A   There were quiet times when the flock was peaceful and David could play his harp. David liked being a shepherd.

B   Sometimes, when everything was quiet, he made up songs to sing to the music of his harp.

A   One day was much like any other—all that changed was the weather.

B   But a day came that was to change David's life. He was sitting in the shade of an overhanging rock when he heard someone running towards him.

A   He jumped up, shaded his eyes against the sun, and saw that it was his oldest brother, Eliab.

B   'Wake up, David,' shouted Eliab, out of breath from running up the hill. 'Dad wants you—now! I'm taking over from you as shepherd.'

A   'Whatever for?' asked David. It had to be serious if Eliab was taking over as shepherd. Eliab and sheep didn't usually go together.

B   'I can hardly believe it—but the prophet from Ramah wants to see you,' panted Eliab. 'Don't ask me why—I don't know. By the way, try and have a wash on the way back home.'

A   It was a long way back to their home in Bethlehem. It gave David a chance to think about the visitor. Whatever did a prophet want with him?

B   He dunked his face in a stream and tried to tidy himself before reaching the farm. Apart from Eliab, all six of his brothers were standing waiting by Jesse his father. They were all looking very serious. Sitting on a rock was an old man.

A   It was Samuel—the prophet from Ramah. Samuel took one glance at David. As he did so, the Lord spoke to him.

B   'He's the one! Get up and pour the olive oil on his head.'

A   Samuel didn't hesitate—well, you don't when God tells you to do something. As David stood, still out of breath, Samuel poured the oil over his head and anointed David to be king.

B Jesse, David's father, and his brothers all looked amazed. Samuel said his goodbyes and returned home to Ramah. His job was done. A new king had been anointed. The only problem was…

A …nobody had told the old king.

Enter King Saul with crown.

B King Saul was the old king. But soon after Saul was made king, things began to go wrong.

Enter Samuel. Saul does not listen to him.

A You see, Saul didn't listen to Samuel and he didn't listen to God. He chose to do his own thing in his own way.

Exit Saul. Enter David, who is anointed by Samuel.

B So when God saw how Saul had disobeyed him, he told Samuel to appoint and anoint a new king. Although David was anointed king, it was to be a long time before he was crowned.

Exit Samuel.

A For the time being, it was back to the sheep for David, killing the wild animals that attacked his flock, and singing his songs.

David exits, leading his flock.

B Then came the day when Jesse, David's father, sent him off with some bread and cheese…

A We'll carry on with the story next time.

B But I want to know what happened with the bread and cheese!

A You'll just have to wait until next time.

⋆ ⋆ ⋆ ⋆ ⋆ **PRAYER** ⋆ ⋆ ⋆ ⋆ ⋆

Loving Father, sometimes we think we are not good enough to do something. Help us to remember that with your help we can do many things. Amen

Reproduced with permission from *Year-round assemblies* published by BRF 2003 (1 84101 328 5)

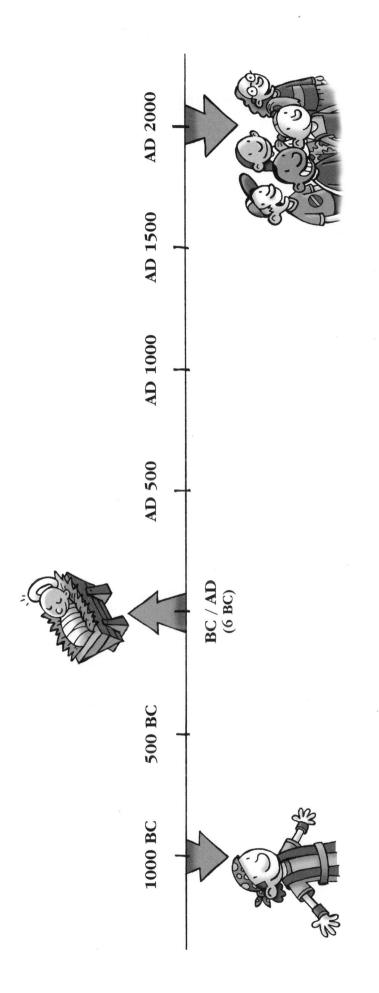

1000 BC   500 BC   BC / AD
                     (6 BC)
                              AD 500   AD 1000   AD 1500   AD 2000

EXTENSION MATERIAL

HYMNS

42 Travel on
45 The journey of life
47 One more step

PSHCE LINKS

Key Stage 1
2a, 2b, 2c, 2e, 3b, 4a, 5c, 5g

Key Stage 2
1a, 2a, 2d, 2e, 2g, 4b, 4e

SUGGESTED ACTIVITIES

 Talk about the various responsibilities a shepherd would have had in David's time. What would the job entail?

 Discuss the choices David had when his brother came to find him. What might have been the outcomes of each decision?

 Discuss why Eliab suggested that David should have a wash on the way home. What preparations might you make if someone important came to your house?

 Draw a picture of David. Around the edge, write the various characteristics that you think he would have possessed, from what you've found out in the story.

 Write a list of similarities and differences between David and yourself. How are your lives, responsibilities and so on similar or different?

 Carry out a 'hot-seat' drama, where Jesse is in the hot seat. What questions might you ask him about how he felt about his youngest son being chosen to be a king? How might he avoid any potential jealousy with David's brothers?

 Act out the story from the assembly. Extend the storyline to show how each character can show their feelings and thoughts.

 Research the various responsibilities that being a king entailed in those days. Would it be a job you would want? Discuss and debate the advantages and disadvantages.

CHAMPION!

 Theme

Facing up to challenges by taking action. Understanding the effects of bullying and making a positive response.

 Aim

To show how one person can make a big difference.

 Bible reference

1 SAMUEL 17:1–50, 55–58

Key verse

1 SAMUEL 17:45

David answered: You've come out to fight me with a sword and a spear and a dagger. But I've come out to fight you in the name of the Lord All-Powerful. He is the God of Israel's army, and you have insulted him too!

 Preparation

You will need cards or OHP acetates showing the response to the following five words in the story. The children respond where indicated by capital letters in the story.

David: 'Our hero'
Israelite(s): 'Hurrah'
Philistines: 'Hiss'
Goliath: 'Oh, no'
Saul: 'Your majesty' (and bow)

****

 CAST

One leader

STORY

Jesse had eight sons. The three older ones were in the ISRAELITE army. They were fighting the PHILISTINES. DAVID was Jesse's youngest son. He was a shepherd. One day Jesse spoke to DAVID.

'Tomorrow, I want you to take some bread and some cheese to your brothers in the ISRAELITE camp. Find out how they are and if they're beating the PHILISTINES.'

DAVID left someone else to look after his sheep. He set out very early in the morning. He reached the ISRAELITE army as the soldiers were taking their places and shouting their battle cry.

It was an exciting place to be. DAVID ran up the battle line looking for his brothers. Just as he found them, there was a great shout from the other side of the valley. It was GOLIATH.

GOLIATH was a PHILISTINE soldier. GOLIATH was about three metres tall. GOLIATH wore a bronze helmet and bronze armour. GOLIATH had a bronze sword strapped to his back and a bronze spear in his hand. A soldier walked in front of GOLIATH, carrying his shield.

'Why are you ISRAELITES lining up for battle?' he shouted. 'I'm the best soldier in the PHILISTINE army. Choose your best soldier to come out and fight me. If he kills me, our people will be your slaves. But if I kill him, you will be our slaves.'

King SAUL and his men heard this shout every morning. They were terrified.

DAVID spoke to some soldiers.

'What will a man get for killing this PHILISTINE?' he asked.

'King SAUL is offering a big reward,' said the ISRAELITE soldiers. 'The man who kills GOLIATH will marry King SAUL'S daughter and never have to pay any more taxes.'

The king heard about DAVID'S questions and sent for him.

'Your majesty,' said DAVID, 'this PHILISTINE shouldn't turn us into cowards. I'll go out and fight him myself.'

'You don't stand a chance,' said King SAUL. 'You're only a boy. GOLIATH has been a soldier all his life.'

'I take care of my father's sheep,' said DAVID. 'When a lion or a bear takes a sheep, I go after it and kill it. I can kill this worthless PHILISTINE. The Lord has kept me safe from lions and bears and he will keep me safe from GOLIATH.'

The king still looked rather doubtful but nobody else in the ISRAELITE army had volunteered.

'Go ahead and fight him,' said King SAUL, 'and may God go with you.'

King SAUL gave DAVID his own personal armour, his helmet and his sword. DAVID put it all on and then found that he had a problem.

'I can't move with all this on,' he said. 'I'm not used to it.'

DAVID took off the armour and then walked down the side of the valley to a small stream. Very carefully he chose five stones. Then, with his sling in one hand and his shepherd's stick in the other, he started to walk towards GOLIATH.

To say the least, the giant was not impressed. Once more a shout echoed around the hills.

'Come on!' roared GOLIATH. 'When I'm finished with you, I'll feed you to the wild animals!'

The ISRAELITE army looked on, terrified. The PHILISTINE soldiers cheered loudly.

'I don't think I can look,' said King SAUL.

DAVID crossed the flat valley bottom and started to climb the side of the valley towards GOLIATH.

'You come against me,' he said, in a voice that could be heard by the soldiers in both camps, 'with a sword and spear. I come to fight you in the name of the Lord All-Powerful. He is the God of ISRAEL'S army. Today the Lord will help me defeat you. Then the whole world will know that ISRAEL has a real God.'

By this time, GOLIATH was quivering with

Reproduced with permission from *Year-round assemblies* published by BRF 2003 (1 84101 328 5)

GOLIATH. It landed with deadly accuracy in the middle of the giant's forehead. GOLIATH fell to the ground with an earth-shaking thud.

The PHILISTINES turned and ran. The ISRAELITES cheered their new hero and chased after the fleeing PHILISTINES.

When it was all over, King SAUL demanded to see DAVID.

'Who are you?' asked the king.

'I am DAVID, the son of Jesse, a loyal ISRAELITE from Bethlehem,' came the reply.

From that moment onward, King SAUL knew very well who DAVID was. Their paths were to cross many times.

anger. The valley trembled as he thundered down towards DAVID. The shepherd boy and the giant were on a collision course. There could be only one winner!

DAVID felt the stones he had chosen from the stream. One was perfect. With the stone in his sling, he whirled it round and round. As he let go of one end, the stone sped like a bullet towards

★ ★ ★ ★ ★ **PRAYER** ★ ★ ★ ★ ★

Loving God, just as David didn't turn and run from what faced him, give us courage and common sense when we have to sort out giant problems. Help us to know that you are with us in all we do. Amen

Reproduced with permission from *Year-round assemblies* published by BRF 2003 (1 84101 328 5)

EXTENSION MATERIAL

HYMNS

45   The journey of life
46   My faith it is an oaken staff
47   One more step
50   When a knight won his spurs

PSHCE LINKS

Key Stage 1
1c, 2c, 2f, 5g

Key Stage 2
1b, 1c, 1e, 2c, 2d, 2f, 4d, 4f, 5g, 5i

SUGGESTED ACTIVITIES

 Talk about the characteristics that David displayed in the story—for example, courage, inquisitiveness, optimism.

 Discuss why King Saul didn't believe that David could make a difference.

 Discuss things that have happened (in school or church, for example) where one person has done something that has made a difference. (This could be either positive or negative.)

 Discuss why we need to be aware of the implications of our actions. For example, they create a certain impression of us. Is this the impression we want people to have?

 Write an imagined conversation between King Saul and David. It could start where David approaches the king and points out that Goliath shouldn't turn the Israelites into cowards. How does Saul react? What kind of things would he say?

 Draw a cartoon strip of the story. Use speech bubbles to record significant parts of the conversation.

 Is fighting the answer? Act out a scene based around an issue that is current for you that involves some element of fighting. Afterwards, discuss the implications of what has happened. How could the situation be resolved in other ways?

IN AND OUT OF FAVOUR

Theme

There are ways of dealing with aggression, our own and other people's. Jealousy can fuel aggression.

Aim

To show how David fell out of favour with Saul but gained favour with God.

Bible reference

1 SAMUEL 16:14–23; 18:6–19, 23

Key verses

1 SAMUEL 18:14–15

The Lord helped David, and he and his soldiers always won their battles. This made Saul even more afraid of David.

Preparation

No specific preparations are required for this assembly.

★ ★

CAST

Six narrators
Chorus of girls
King Saul
David
Jesse (David's father)
Princess Michal
Court officials

STORY

SCENE ONE

Narrator 1	King Saul was not a happy man.
Narrator 2	King Saul was a very unhappy man.
Narrator 3	King Saul was a frightened man.
Narrator 1	He was jumpy…
Narrator 2	…and bad tempered…
Narrator 3	…and needed help.
Narrator 2	Music is what you need, your Majesty.
Narrator 1	Music will make you feel better, your Majesty.
Narrator 3	'All right,' said the king. 'Find me someone who can play the harp. Then bring him here. He had better be really good.'
Narrator 2	'I happen to know someone who is an excellent player,' said a court official. 'He's the son of Jesse. The family live in Bethlehem. This boy is brave and good-looking, speaks well *and* the Lord is with him.'
Narrator 1	A few days later, Jesse was very surprised to get a message from King Saul.
Narrator 2	And so was David!
Narrator 3	'Listen to me, son,' said Jesse. 'You're going to the king. It might

Narrator 2 Can't be the same as the way I play. My playing doesn't make anyone relax and feel better!

Change narrators.

SCENE TWO

Narrator 4 So, for a time, all went well. Then there was a giant of a problem.

Narrator 5 A giant by the name of Goliath.

Narrator 6 As you heard last time, David killed Goliath.

Narrator 4 This made a big impression on King Saul.

Narrator 5 And quite a big impression on the giant!

Narrator 6 The problem was this…

Split chorus of girls into two groups, A and B: They say the following pair of lines three times—each time getting louder than the one before.

Group A Saul has killed a thousand enemies.

Group B David has killed TEN thousand enemies.

Narrator 4 This song made King Saul very angry indeed.

be a good idea if you took one or two things with you.'

Narrator 2 David took some bread, quite a lot of wine, a donkey and a young goat.

Narrator 1 Saul liked the look of David…

Narrator 3 …and the bread, wine, donkey and goat!

Narrator 2 So David left his father's sheep and started to work for King Saul.

Narrator 1 Very soon he was promoted. King Saul made David his armour bearer. He had to carry the king's…

Narrator 3 …sword…

Narrator 1 …spear…

Narrator 2 …and shield.

Narrator 3 Not long after this, Jesse got another message from the king.

Narrator 1 'I really like David. Please let him stay with me,' said the message.

Narrator 2 Well, you don't argue with the king, so David stayed and someone else looked after the sheep.

Narrator 3 Whenever King Saul had one of his bad moods, David played for him.

Narrator 1 The music made Saul relax and feel better.

25

Reproduced with permission from *Year-round assemblies* published by BRF 2003 (1 84101 328 5)

Narrator 5	'They say David has killed ten times more than I have,' roared the king. 'Next thing, they will want to make him king.'
Narrator 6	This was quite funny. If you remember, David had already been secretly anointed king by old Samuel.
Narrator 4	Shush. Don't let Saul know that, whatever you do.

Narrator 6	Then Saul had one of his really bad moods. He was ranting and raving and waving a spear around.
Narrator 4	They sent for David. He started to play his harp.
Narrator 5	Saul lifted the spear and…
Narrator 6	…hurled it at David. Not once but twice.
Narrator 4	David just managed to dodge the spear and escape from the house.

Change narrators.

Narrator 2	Saul knew that God was with David because David kept winning battles against the old enemy…
Narrator 3	…the Philistines. One day Saul had a cunning plan.
Narrator 1	Saul was good at cunning plans. This one was *very* cunning.
Narrator 2	Saul thought to himself, 'I don't want to kill David myself. It wouldn't go down too well with the people. So what if…
Narrator 3	…I get the Philistines to do it for me? Perfect.'
Narrator 1	Now Saul had a daughter called Princess Michal…
Narrator 2	…who was beautiful…
Narrator 3	…who was madly in love with David…
Narrator 1	…who wanted to marry him.
Narrator 2	But what about Saul's cunning plan?
Narrator 3	One of Saul's officials told David, 'The Princess is yours to marry if you will kill one hundred Philistines for the king.'
Narrator 1	'Hopefully,' planned Saul, 'David will get killed by the Philistines instead.'
Narrator 2	But David killed not one hundred but two hundred Philistines so King Saul had to…
Narrator 3	…let Princess Michal marry David.
Narrator 1	And they all lived happily ever after.
Narrators 2, 3, 4, 5, 6	Oh no, they didn't!

SCENE THREE

Narrator 1	That was a close thing. But Saul now knew that God was helping David, and that made King Saul afraid.

EXTENSION MATERIAL

HYMNS

43   Give me oil in my lamp
45   The journey of life
56   The Lord's my shepherd
59   The best gift

PSHCE LINKS

Key Stage 1
1a, 2b, 4a, 4c, 5g

Key Stage 1
1a, 2c, 2e, 2f, 3f, 4b, 5c

SUGGESTED ACTIVITIES

 Talk about whether Saul's actions can be justified. Did he act fairly? Are his actions understandable? How else could he have acted?

 Discuss how Saul's demands put David in a difficult position. Was David really given a choice about fighting?

 Discuss being good at something (like David and his harp playing). What different skills can the group come up with? What range of abilities is displayed?

 Talk about David's options. Did he have any choice when Saul asked him to come to the palace or when he had to go and fight?

 Discuss from the story whether you think Saul was a good king. Were his motives good ones?

 Write an imagined conversation between two courtiers after Saul threw the spear at David. What might they have said? Do you think they would have been surprised?

 Draw a picture of how you think Princess Michal might have looked. Think about what types of clothes and jewellery she might have worn.

 Make up a list of the similarities and differences between Saul and David. What evidence is there to support each characteristic?

 Write a diary account as if it was from David of the story. How would he express his feelings? What range of emotions does the story cover?

★ ★ ★ ★ ★ ★ ★ ★ 【 **4** 】 ★ ★ ★ ★ ★ ★ ★ ★

FRIENDS AND SECRETS

 Theme

A consideration of loyalty and friendship. How do we decide to which friend or cause we should be loyal? What are the effects of loyalty?

 Aim

To show the importance of friends and family.

 Bible reference

1 SAMUEL 19:1–17

 Key verse

1 SAMUEL 19:11

Michal, David's wife, told him, 'If you don't escape tonight, they'll kill you tomorrow!'

 Preparation

Simple clothes for the part of Princess Michal—for example, long dress, shawl and hair ornament.

★ ★

CAST

Narrator
Princess Michal

STORY

Narrator	I'm very pleased to say that we have an important visitor, a member of the royal family, visiting us for our assembly today. She is none other than her royal highness, Princess Michal.
Michal	Thank you, I'm delighted to be here. I believe that you have been hearing about my father King Saul and my husband David.
Narrator	That's right, your highness. May we congratulate you on your recent marriage. We do hope that you will both be very happy.

Michal	Thank you, but I'm sorry to say that things are not too good at the moment. David has done so well fighting the Philistines that Dad has become rather jealous. You know what men are like.
Narrator	You have a brother, don't you? How does he get on with David?
Michal	You mean Jonathan? Jonathan and David are very good friends. They met just after David killed that Philistine monster, Goliath. In fact, Jonathan liked David so much that he gave him his own sword.
Narrator	So David has at least got one friend at court. It must be very difficult for you all. Does your father still have these really frightening angry moods?
Michal	He certainly does. David was playing the harp for my father only the other night. Suddenly his whole mood changed. He grabbed a spear and flung it at David.
Narrator	Whatever happened? Is David all right?
Michal	Thankfully, David managed to dodge the spear. He ran out of Saul's house and came straight home.
Narrator	That must have been terrifying for you both!
Michal	It certainly was! But it was even worse than that. You see, David thought he had been followed. He told me to look out of the window. In the shadows I could see soldiers hiding. I knew they were there waiting to kill David in the morning.
Narrator	So David was in the house just waiting to be killed when the dawn came?
Michal	Well, yes. It was then that I had an idea. Our house is built into the

	town wall. The soldiers were at the front inside the wall. I found a rope, tied it to the window, and told David to climb down. I watched as he ran off in the dark.
Narrator	But what about the soldiers in the morning?
Michal	I needed to give David as much time as possible to escape. I put a sort of statue in our bed, put some goat hair on top, and dressed it in some of David's clothes. When the soldiers came, I told them that David was unwell. They had one look and went off to tell the king.
Narrator	So you played this trick on the soldiers? But did King Saul believe you?
Michal	No, my father's too smart for that. He sent the soldiers back and ordered them to bring David to him. They pulled the clothes off the bed and found the statue and goat's hair. There were some red-faced soldiers that morning!
Narrator	So you gave David lots of time to get away, but where did he go?
Michal	Perhaps you remember that Samuel had anointed David as the

Reproduced with permission from *Year-round assemblies* published by BRF 2003 (1 84101 328 5)

next king? Well, David went off to see him. He told Samuel what King Saul had done. Then Saul heard where David was and set off after him.

Narrator What does your brother Jonathan feel about all this?

Michal Jonathan cannot understand why Dad wants to kill David. After all, David is the best soldier we have. David escaped from the king once more and he went straight to Jonathan.

Narrator Did Jonathan help David?

Michal At first, Jonathan didn't believe that Saul wanted to kill David. David told him how close to death he had been but Jonathan still found it hard to believe that his father would want to kill his best friend. It all came clear to Jonathan at the Festival of the New Moon.

Narrator Surely David didn't go to the festival?

Michal No, he didn't. But he did hide in a field near to where Saul and Jonathan were eating. Sadly, Saul and Jonathan had a big argument. Saul blamed Jonathan for the fact that David wasn't there and called him a traitor for taking David's side.

Narrator So your brother was in trouble as well as your husband.

Michal Yes. Saul lost his temper again. This time he even threw a spear at Jonathan. Well, that was enough for Jonathan. He left the table and went out. The next morning he met David in his secret hiding spot. They hugged each other and then said goodbye. David knew he had to get away. It was a very sad moment for them both.

Narrator But what did David do? Where did he go?

Michal I'm afraid I can't tell you. You see, I must keep it a secret from the king. I'm sorry but I must go now. I'm sure you'll find out soon.

Narrator Thank you, Princess Michal, for telling us more about David. May the Lord keep you both safe.

★ ★ ★ ★ ★ **PRAYER** ★ ★ ★ ★ ★

Jesus, friend and brother, thank you for all our friends. Help us not just to be friends with people we like, but also to be friendly towards those who are unhappy and lonely. Amen

Reproduced with permission from *Year-round assemblies* published by BRF 2003 (1 84101 328 5)

EXTENSION MATERIAL

HYMNS

53 Peace, perfect peace
57 Lost and found
65 When I needed a neighbour
70 Cross over the road
89 Guess how I feel

PSHCE LINKS

Key Stage 1
1a, 2a, 2b, 4d, 5g

Key Stage 2
1a, 2a, 2c, 2d, 2e, 2f, 4b, 4c, 5g

SUGGESTED ACTIVITIES

 Devise a further list of questions to ask Princess Michal. Can you imagine how she might answer?

 Discuss the actions of the Princess. Where do her loyalties lie? Do you think she had an easy decision to make? What might happen to her now?

 Talk about the qualities of Jonathan. What makes him a good friend?

 Fold a piece of paper. On one half, write the reasons why the princess should support her father. On the other half, write the reasons why she should support her husband. This could then form the basis of a debate.

 Write down an imaginary conversation between Princess Michal and Jonathan.

 Create a drama around your work with the interview questions for the Princess. You could act out the assembly for yourself and then add on the extended part that you have written.

 Act out the conversation between Michal and Jonathan. Remember to get plenty of emotion into it to make it believable!

 Research the expectations of women at the time. How does this affect your opinion of the princess and the way she chose to act?

HIDE AND SEEK

 Theme

Making the right decisions is not always straightforward. Different values and customs may affect our decisions.

 Aim

To show how God kept David safe through all his adventures.

 Bible reference

1 SAMUEL 22—24; 26:1–25

 Key verse

1 SAMUEL 26:23

'The Lord put you in my power today, but you are his chosen king and I wouldn't harm you. The Lord rewards people who are faithful and live right.'

 Preparation

Scene One: David and his supporters are on stage.
Scene Two: Saul and his supporters are on stage.
Scene Three: Both David and Saul are on stage, plus some of their supporters.

★ ★

CAST

Nine narrators
David with a sword
Saul wearing a crown
David's supporters
Saul's supporters

STORY

SCENE ONE

David comes on stage.

Narrator 1 We left David running off after he'd said goodbye to Jonathan, the son of King Saul.

Narrator 2 David knew that his life was in danger. King Saul wanted to kill him and David had to run for his life.

Narrator 3 He went first to the town of Nob to see Ahimelech the priest. Unfortunately there was…

Narrator 1 …a spy in Nob. The spy was Doeg. And Doeg saw David.

Narrator 2 David had a problem. When he saw that Doeg had spotted him, he also realized that he had run away leaving his sword behind.

Narrator 3 Well, you can't be much of a soldier without a sword. So what did he do?

Narrator 1 It just so happened that tucked behind a statue was a rather special sword. It was the sword that used to belong to…

Narrator 2 GOLIATH! You remember him? He was the giant that David killed.

Narrator 3 Ahimelech the priest said to David…

Narrator 1   'You were the one who killed Goliath, so you can take his sword.'

Narrator 2   So David now had a sword, but it wasn't safe to stay in Nob. For one thing, Doeg, the spy, knew he was there.

Enter David's supporters.

Narrator 4   David kept running away from King Saul. It wasn't safe to stay in towns so he went to live in a cave.

Narrator 5   Some of his family heard he was there. They joined David in the cave along with about four hundred other people who also felt outcast for one reason or another.

SCENE TWO

Exit David and his supporters. Enter Saul and his supporters.

Narrator 6   But what was King Saul up to?

Narrator 4   Probably up to no good, I should think!

Narrator 5   He was telling off his officers.

Narrator 6   'You never warned me that my own son Jonathan had helped David. You're all plotting against me.'

Narrator 4   Doeg, the spy, was standing with the other officers.

Narrator 5   'When I was in the town of Nob, I saw David,' said Doeg. 'He was visiting Ahimelech the priest. Ahimelech gave David food and the sword that belonged to Goliath.'

Narrator 6   'Send Ahimelech and his fellow priests to me,' ordered King Saul.

Narrator 4   Ahimelech came to the king. He told Saul that David was loyal to the king. But Saul got in a rage and…

Narrator 5   …I'm sorry to say, he had Ahimelech and all his priests killed.

Narrator 6   But one person escaped. He was Ahimelech's son, Abiathar.

Narrator 4   Abiathar ran to the only person who could save him…

Exit Saul and his supporters. Enter David and his supporters.

SCENE THREE

Narrator 7   …David. David was not too surprised when he heard what Saul had done.

Narrator 8   'When I saw that spy, Doeg, I knew he would tell Saul,' said David. 'Abiathar, your family died because of me. Stay with me and you will be safe.'

Narrator 9   David and his men had to move from place to place, as King Saul was chasing them.

Narrator 7   Once, David and his men were going round a hill on one side and…

Reproduced with permission from *Year-round assemblies* published by BRF 2003 (1 84101 328 5)

Enter Saul and his supporters.

Narrator 8 …King Saul and his men were going round the other side. Saul was just about to capture David when a messenger came to say…

Narrator 9 'Come quickly! The Philistines are attacking us and taking everything.'

Narrator 7 Saul had to stop chasing David and fight the Philistines instead.

Narrator 8 After defeating the Philistines, King Saul set off again after David. This time he had three thousand of the best soldiers with him.

David and Saul stand on opposite sides of the stage with their respective supporters.

Narrator 9 Spies told Saul that David was hiding in the desert near Jeshimon. Saul set up his camp on a hilltop nearby.

Narrator 7 When night fell, David crept into the middle of King Saul's camp. He found Saul sleeping. Next to Saul, stuck in the ground, was the king's spear. Next to the spear was Abner, Saul's best soldier.

Narrator 8 David killed King Saul with his own spear.

Narrator 9 Well, actually he didn't. It must have been very tempting. But David knew that Saul's life was in God's hands, not his.

Narrator 7 David took the spear…

Narrator 8 …and Saul's water bottle…

Narrator 9 …and crept very quietly away from the camp.

Narrator 7 When he reached the top of the next hill…

Narrator 8 …David shouted to Abner…

Narrator 9 … 'Abner, what kind of a man are you? You're a failure. See if you can find the king's spear and his water jar.'

Narrator 7 By now, King Saul was awake. He knew how easily David could have killed him.

Narrator 8 'I'll never try to harm you again,' shouted Saul across the valley. 'Please come back.'

Narrator 9 But David knew better than to trust King Saul. He said a lovely thing…

Narrator 7 … 'The Lord put you in my power today, but you are his chosen king and I wouldn't harm you. The Lord rewards people who are faithful and live right.'

Narrator 8 King Saul went back home.

Narrator 9 David also left, but he thought to himself, 'One of these days, Saul is going to kill me.'

Exit David and Saul plus their supporters.

⋆ ⋆ ⋆ ⋆ ⋆ **PRAYER** ⋆ ⋆ ⋆ ⋆ ⋆

Loving God, sometimes we are afraid. Help us to share our fear with you and give us the courage to stand up to our fears. Amen

EXTENSION MATERIAL

HYMNS

60 I listen and I listen
85 Spirit of peace
87 Give us hope, Lord
92 When night arrives
93 Morning sun

PSHCE LINKS

Key Stage 1
2a, 2b, 2c, 4d, 5g

Key Stage 2
1a, 2a, 2c, 2e, 4a, 4b

SUGGESTED ACTIVITIES

 Discuss the trust and loyalty that must have been instilled into the family of David and Micah and his soldiers, that they were allowed to know where David was hiding.

 Talk about how Saul's officers would have felt as Saul told them off and accused them of plotting against him.

 Discuss how Saul would have felt on discovering that his son had betrayed him and had helped David.

 Discuss Saul's actions when he killed Ahimelech and the other priests. Was he acting reasonably?

 Write down Saul's reasons for fighting the Philistines, and for fighting David. Which would you battle against in his position?

 Write a diary entry for David, describing how he crept into Saul's tent and took his spear and water bottle. Remember to use as many senses as you can and to use effective adjectives to create a real feeling of tension.

 Write a character profile of Saul using the information you have found out so far. What are his good and bad features?

 Play the bear and the honey-pot game. (A person in the middle of a circle is blindfolded, with a set of keys lying near to them. Other people take turns to creep up on them and steal the keys without making a sound and return to their place. If the person in the middle hears them, and points accurately, they have to go back to their place and wait for another turn.)

KING AT LAST

 Theme

Dealing with our feelings about the loss of those we love—relations, friends, pets. Also looking at how patience is often needed before we achieve a particular goal.

 Aim

To show how Saul died and David became king.

 Bible reference

2 SAMUEL 5

Key verse

2 SAMUEL 5:4

David was thirty years old when he became king, and he ruled for forty years.

 Preparation

There is a short interactive section in the middle of the narration for which the following responses are required:

- King David: 'Our hero'
- Jebusites: 'Boo'
- Victory: 'Hurrah'

★★

CAST

Two leaders/narrators (A and B)

STORY

A King Saul never did catch David. The battles against the Philistines continued and the time came when the Philistines defeated Saul's army.

B They killed three of the king's sons, including David's best friend, Jonathan. Saul was badly wounded by enemy arrows and, rather than fall into Philistine hands, he took his own life by falling on his sword.

A Three days after the battle, a soldier from Saul's army reached David. David questioned him.

B 'Who won the battle?' asked David.

A 'Our army turned and ran,' said the soldier, 'but many were wounded and died. Even King Saul and his son Jonathan are dead.'

B David was heartbroken at the news of Jonathan's death. He wrote a song in memory of Saul and Jonathan and ordered the whole nation to learn it. The song was called 'The Song of the Bow'. The song starts:

A 'Israel, your famous hero lies dead on the hills, and your mighty warriors have fallen.'

B The song finishes on a very sad note.

A 'Jonathan, I miss you most! I loved you like a brother. You were truly loyal to me, and more faithful than a wife to her husband. Our warriors have fallen, and their weapons are destroyed.'

B After the death of Saul, David met the leaders of Israel.

A 'The Lord God has promised that you would rule our country and take care of us like a shepherd,' they told David. 'We have come to crown you king of Israel.'

B They poured olive oil on David's head to show that he was now king. David must have remembered how old Samuel had poured oil on his head all those years before.

A At last Samuel's promise had come true. David was thirty years old when he became king of Israel. He was to be king for forty years.

INTERACTIVE SECTION

Children respond to the names in capital letters.

B Now every king needs a palace. But if you are going to build a palace, then you need a good city in which to build it—a city that can be defended against the enemy.

A Jerusalem was the city KING DAVID wanted. There was only one problem—it belonged to the JEBUSITES. The JEBUSITES were yet another of the tribes against whom KING DAVID was fighting.

B The JEBUSITES jeered. 'Even if we couldn't walk and couldn't see, we could drive you away. You'll never get in here!'

A That really annoyed KING DAVID. It was enough to make him determined to capture the city. Then he had a brilliant idea. He would lose hundreds of men if he attacked from the outside. The city walls were steep; his men would have no chance.

B But what if he attacked from the inside? There was just one chance—the water staircase. A staircase ran from inside the city to a stream which flowed just outside the city wall.

A KING DAVID waited until the JEBUSITES were asleep. His men climbed the staircase. It wasn't easy to be quiet with swords, spears and shields, but they made it to the top. Then they were there in the centre of Jerusalem.

B The JEBUSITES didn't know what hit them.

A Most were still asleep.

B KING DAVID's men caught them totally unprepared.

A The VICTORY was complete.

B From that moment, Jerusalem has had a

Reproduced with permission from *Year-round assemblies* published by BRF 2003 (1 84101 328 5)

second name—the City of David. The king had his city and soon he would have his palace. He ordered carpenters and stone masons, and work on the building of the palace began.

End of interaction.

A David hadn't finished. There was something else he wanted to bring into his city—something very important, something that was very holy.

B It was the Ark of the Covenant.

A The Ark of the Covenant was a sacred chest made from acacia wood. The chest was covered in gold.

B Inside the box were the two tablets of the Ten Commandments, given to Moses by God hundreds of years before. At each end of the box were figures of angels.

A The Ark of the Covenant was a symbol of God's protection. It was sometimes carried into battle to remind the Israelites that God was with them. David wanted to take God's Ark to his city. So important was this that he brought together thirty thousand of Israel's finest soldiers.

B Everyone was celebrating.

A David was dancing with excitement.

B The people were cheering and…

A …blowing horns as the sacred chest passed by.

B The procession went into the city, where they put the chest inside a tent that David had put up for it. There was more music and dancing. David worshipped the Lord God and then blessed the people. David was so happy that the Ark of the Covenant was now in his city.

A The new palace was finished and the king moved in. For a time the kingdom was at peace. But there was trouble just over the horizon.

★ ★ ★ ★ ★ **PRAYER** ★ ★ ★ ★ ★

Father God, waiting is always hard. Sometimes we are impatient—we want things to happen now. Help us to learn that sometimes it is better to wait a little longer. Amen

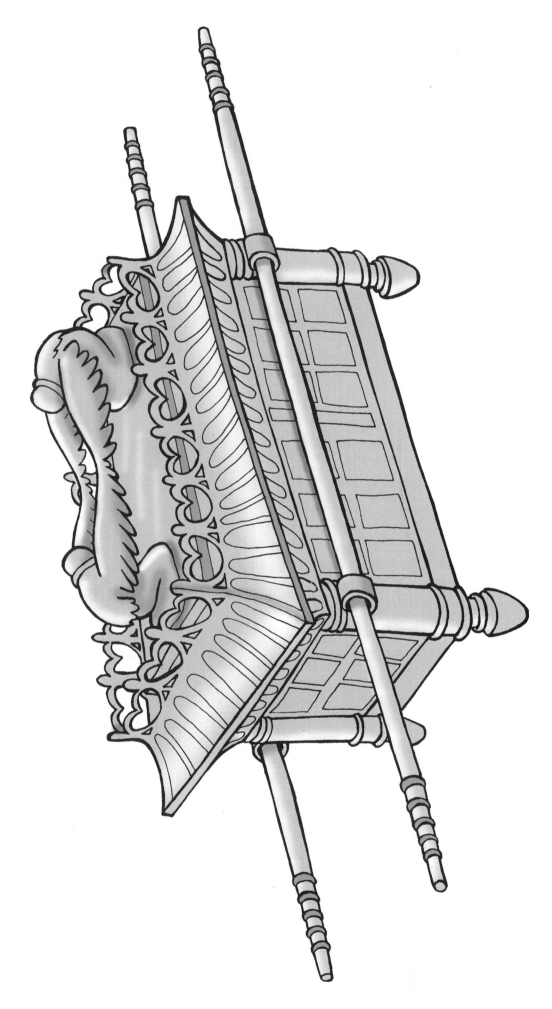

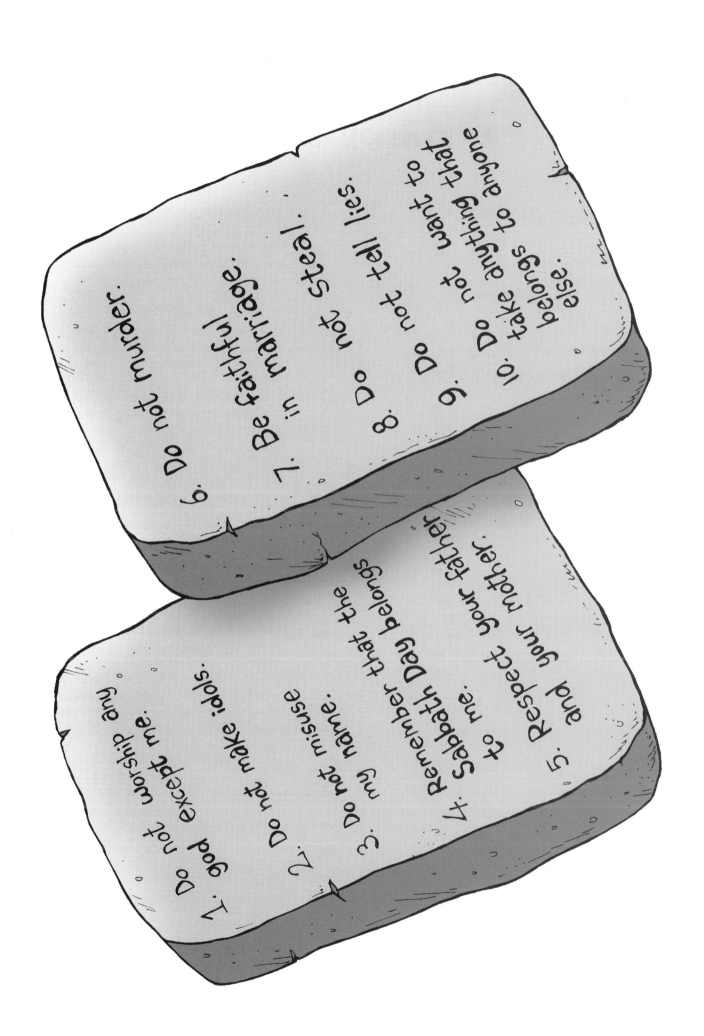

1. Do not worship any god except me.
2. Do not make idols.
3. Do not misuse my name.
4. Remember that the Sabbath Day belongs to me.
5. Respect your father and your mother.
6. Do not murder.
7. Be faithful in marriage.
8. Do not steal.
9. Do not tell lies.
10. Do not want to take anything that belongs to anyone else.

EXTENSION MATERIAL

HYMNS

30　Join with us
31　God has promised
33　Praise the Lord
35　Praise the Lord, you heavens
40　Praise Him

PSHCE LINKS

Key Stage 1
1c, 2a, 5b

Key Stage 2
1a, 2b, 2e, 4b, 4c

SUGGESTED ACTIVITIES

 Discuss how David felt when he heard that Saul had been defeated, and contrast this with the news of Jonathan's death.

 Talk about the mixed feelings David must have had when he was made king. What responsibilities would it have involved at that time? Would it have been an easy job?

 Discuss why the Ark of the Covenant was so important to David. What significance did the Ten Commandments have for David? Discuss how significant they are in today's society.

 Draw how you imagine the city of Jerusalem might have looked with David's army surrounding it.

 Draw the Ark of the Covenant. Remember, it was made of acacia wood and covered in gold, with angel figures at each end. Do you think it would have had jewels on as well?

 Write your own set of rules and compare them to the Ten Commandments. Why are rules important? Why do we still need them today?

 David is known for his ability to write songs. Try your hand at writing a poem or a piece of prose about something that has made a big impression on you.

 Read the whole of 'The Song of the Bow' (2 Samuel 1:17–27).

THE KING TAKES A WIFE

 Theme

Our behaviour does not only affect ourselves but other people too. Pressure to behave in an unacceptable way can come from many directions.

 Aim

To show how, despite David's love of God, he gave in to temptation.

Bible reference

2 SAMUEL 11:1—12:25

> **Key verse**
>
> 2 SAMUEL 12:13
> *David said, 'I have disobeyed the Lord.'*

✂ **Preparation**

No specific preparation is needed.

★★★★★★★★★★★★★★★★★★★★★★★★★★★★★★★★★★

CAST

Two leaders / narrators (A and B)

STORY

A We warned you, in the last story about King David, that trouble was brewing.

B But David had just been made king. He had just made Jerusalem his capital city. Surely nothing could go wrong?

A It wasn't so much that things went wrong but that David went wrong. Although he was king, that didn't stop him from doing something that was very wrong. It happened like this…

B   One day David woke up after his siesta.

A   What's a siesta?

B   It usually means having a sleep in the middle of the day.

A   So David woke up…

B   …and went for a walk around the flat roof of his palace.

A   Get a lovely view from there.

B   That was the problem. David had a lovely view but it wasn't the countryside. It was of a beautiful lady in the courtyard of another house.

A   Well, David was knocked over by the beauty of this woman. He had to know who she was. He sent one of his servants to find out her name.

B   'Her name, your Majesty, is Bathsheba. Her husband is Uriah.'

A   And that was the problem. The beautiful Bathsheba was a married woman.

B   So David forgot Bathsheba?

A   Well, no, he didn't. He sent a message to Bathsheba inviting her round to the palace for the evening. Well, you can't very well say no to a king—so she came.

B   So what was the problem?

A   A month or two later, Bathsheba found out that she was going to have a baby. AND… David, the king, was the father.

B   So it was David who was the father of Bathsheba's baby and not Uriah, her husband?

A   That's right. From then on, things just got worse for David. They often do when we try to hide the wrong things we do.

B   Well, come on, tell me what happened.

A   David's army was away from Jerusalem fighting the Ammonites. Now Uriah was a soldier, a very brave soldier. He was with the army…

B   …fighting the Ammonites!

A   David did a very mean thing. He sent a message to General Joab, who was commanding David's army. The message went like this…

B   'Put Uriah in the front line where the fighting is worst. Then pull the troops back from him, so that he will be wounded and die.'

A   And that was what happened. Uriah, the brave soldier, the husband of Bathsheba, was killed because of David's orders.

B   That was a very bad thing to do. That's often what happens, though. You do something wrong and then do something even worse to try to get out of trouble. It never works.

A   God was very unhappy at the way David had treated Uriah. He sent Nathan the prophet to see David. Nathan told David a story.

B   That's a strange thing to do.

A   Not really. You see, we can all learn from stories. The story that Nathan told was about a rich man and a poor man.

B   The rich man had lots of sheep and cows…

A   …he was very rich.

B   The poor man only had one lamb…

A   …he was very poor.

B   One day, a visitor came to lunch with the rich man.

A   Not wanting to kill one of his own sheep, the rich man…

B … 'It's you! God made you king, he kept you safe, he gave you everything. But you took Uriah's wife and you took Uriah's life…

A …You are just like the man in the story.'

B That must have made David really think about what he had done.

A Yes, Nathan's story helped David to understand that what he had done was very wrong. He was very sorry.

B But what happened to the baby?

A The baby was born—a little boy. Sadly, though, the baby didn't live very long.

B Did David and Bathsheba have any more children?

A Yes, they had a son called Solomon. Solomon became king after David.

B …stole the poor man's lamb…

A …and killed it…

B …and gave it to his visitor for supper.

A The story made David very, very angry.

B 'Nathan,' said David, 'tell me who this rich man is. He deserves to die!'

A And Nathan pointed his finger at David and said…

★ ★ ★ ★ ★ **PRAYER** ★ ★ ★ ★ ★

Lord God, we make many mistakes. Help us to say sorry and then to learn not to make the same mistake again. Amen

EXTENSION MATERIAL

HYMNS

48 Father, hear the prayer we offer
51 The Lord's prayer
52 Lord of all hopefulness
63 Spirit of God
91 Break out

PSHCE LINKS

Key Stage 1
1a, 1b, 2a, 2b, 2c, 4a, 5g

Key Stage 2
1a, 2a, 2b, 2c, 2e, 2f, 4a, 4b

SUGGESTED ACTIVITIES

 Discuss the actions of David. Was he justified? What influenced the way he acted? Does being a king make him 'invincible'?

 Discuss how God must have felt as he watched what David was doing.

 How do you think Bathsheba must have felt? Were her feelings taken into consideration? Would this kind of action happen in today's Western society?

 Discuss which of the Ten Commandments David broke. Talk about what happens when society doesn't have rules, or when people don't abide by the rules that are established.

 Write down as many points of view as you can think of, from what happened in the story. What effect would David's actions have had on the people living in Jerusalem at the time?

 Construct a hot-seat situation, with different characters taking the parts of David, Uriah and Bathsheba.

 Research the customs of David's time, particularly looking at the structure of a family. How does it differ from today? What advantages and disadvantages are associated with men having many wives?

SONGS AND PSALMS

 Theme
A celebration of talents—the importance of developing a talent and using it.

 Aim
To show the different aspects of David's character.

 Bible reference
PSALMS 23; 101; 103; 108

 Key verse
PSALM 101:1
I will sing to you, Lord! I will celebrate your kindness and your justice.

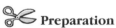 **Preparation**
There are four scenes, each requiring two readers. The following four titles for David should be printed on to card and held up at the appropriate time.

- Shepherd
- Musician
- King
- A man who loved God

★ ★

CAST

Two narrators
David (the character of David may be played by four different children)
Saul, holding a spear

STORY

SCENE ONE

Narrator 1 David was king of Israel for forty years. Before David took up his role as king, he was a fearless shepherd.

Enter David the shepherd with a sheep.

Narrator 1 This is a song that David wrote to God, comparing him to a wonderful shepherd.

Narrator 2 You, Lord, are my shepherd. I will never be in need. You let me rest in fields of green grass. You lead me to streams of peaceful water, and you refresh my life. You are true to your name, and you lead me along the right paths. I may walk through valleys as dark as death, but I won't be afraid. You are with me, and your shepherd's rod makes me feel safe. You treat me to a feast, while my enemies watch. You honour me as a guest, and you fill my cup until it overflows. Your kindness and love will always be with me each day of my life, and I will live for ever in your house, Lord. (Psalm 23)

SCENE TWO

Narrator 1 As well as being a fearless shepherd, David was also a brilliant musician.

Enter David the musician with a harp.

Narrator 1 This is a song that David wrote about his music. He tried to help King Saul when one of his dark moods came over him.

Enter Saul, holding a spear.

Narrator 2 Our God, I am faithful to you with all my heart, and you can trust me. I will sing and play music for you with all that I am. I will start playing my harps before the sun rises. I will praise you, Lord, for everyone to hear; I will sing hymns to you in every nation. Your love reaches higher than the heavens, and your loyalty extends beyond the clouds. Our God, may you be honoured above the heavens; may your glory be seen everywhere on earth. (Psalm 108:1–5)

SCENE THREE

Narrator 1 As well as being a fine musician, David was a very great king.

Enter David as king.

Narrator 1 This is a song that David wrote about being a king.

Narrator 2 I will sing to you, Lord! I will celebrate your kindness and your justice. Please help me learn to do the right thing, and I will be honest and fair in my own kingdom. I refuse to be corrupt or to take part in anything crooked, and I won't be dishonest or deceitful. Anyone who spreads gossip will be silenced, and no one who is conceited will be my friend. I will find trustworthy people to serve as my advisers, and only an honest person will serve as an official. No one who cheats or lies will have a position in my royal court. I will sing to you, Lord! I will celebrate your kindness and your justice. (Psalm 101:1–7)

SCENE FOUR

Narrator 1 As well as being a very great king, David was also a man who loved God and knew that even when he had done wrong, God loved him too.

Enter David, who kneels down.

Narrator 1 This is a song that David wrote about God.

Narrator 2 With all my heart I praise the Lord, and with all that I am I praise his holy name! With all my heart I praise the Lord! I will never forget how kind he has been. The Lord forgives our sins, heals us when we are sick, and protects us from death. His kindness and love are a crown on our heads. Each day that we live, he provides for our needs and gives us the strength of a young eagle. The Lord is merciful! He is kind and patient, and his love never fails. (Psalm 103:1–5, 8)

Narrator 1 David was a shepherd boy, a musician, a great king and a man who loved God. We thank God for what we can learn from the life of David.

★ ★ ★ ★ ★ **PRAYER** ★ ★ ★ ★ ★

We will sing to you, Lord! We will celebrate your kindness and justice. Please help us to learn to do the right thing, and to be honest and fair. Amen

EXTENSION MATERIAL

HYMNS

30 Join with us
31 God has promised
32 Thank you, Lord
33 Praise the Lord in everything
40 Praise Him

PSHCE LINKS

Key Stage 1
1d, 2a, 2f, 2h, 4a, 5b, 5f

Key Stage 2
1b, 4a, 4b, 5b

SUGGESTED ACTIVITIES

 Take turns with a friend, telling them all the things you are good at. Report back to the rest of the group what your friend is good at. (You will have to listen carefully!)

 Talk to someone in the group whom you don't normally associate with. How many things can you find out about them that you didn't know before? Do you have anything in common that you didn't realize?

 Discuss what type of faith David must have had. How can you support your findings?

 Write down the things you do well and try to make them into a rhyme. You could later try to add a tune so that it becomes a song.

 Have a go at writing a prayer or a piece of writing, thanking God for all the different things you can do.

 Write down the different qualities needed to be a good shepherd, king, musician and follower of God. Which attributes are needed for all of them and which are specific to the job?

 Research some of the psalms that David wrote. What are the main themes that David mentions?

JESUS DAVIDSON

 Theme

Family relationships—the responsibilities of belonging to a family. Family traditions. Dealing with problems within a family.

 Aim

To show the link between David and Jesus and between the Old and New Testaments.

 Bible references

MATTHEW 1:1–17; LUKE 1:26–38, 46–48

 Key verse

MATTHEW 1:1
Jesus Christ came from the family of King David.

 Preparation

Card or OHP acetate showing some names that end in the suffix 'son'—for example, Johnson, Robinson, Thompson, Robertson and so on.

★ ★

CAST

Two leaders / narrators (A and B)

STORY

A Many people have two sorts of names. They have a first name or Christian name. And then they have a family name or surname. Many family names end in the word 'son'.

Show cards.

B For example, Johnson…
A …or Robertson…
B …or Thompson.
A These names will have originated many years ago. The son of John was called John's son or Johnson.
B In the same way, the sons of Robert and Thomas became Robertson and Thompson.

 Reproduced with permission from *Year-round assemblies* published by BRF 2003 (1 84101 328 5)

A All this term, we have been following the life of David. The stories that we have heard all come from the part of the Bible we call the Old Testament. The books in the Old Testament tell us about the time before Jesus.

B In a few weeks' time, we shall remember the birth of Jesus at Christmas. Today our story takes us from the Old Testament…

A …into the New Testament. It starts with someone we know quite well.

B It starts with David.

A The first book in the New Testament is the gospel of Matthew. The first words in the book of Matthew are these…

B … 'Jesus Christ came from the family of King David.'

A It then goes on to list the family of Jesus from David through to Joseph and Mary, Jesus' parents. The list is Jesus' family tree.

B Many times in the New Testament, Jesus is called Jesus, son of David. So we could actually call him Jesus Davidson.

A Now, just before Christmas we are going to think about Jesus, son of David, and how he came into our world.

B The story begins in the little town of Nazareth with a girl called Mary…

A …and a man called Joseph.

B Joseph and Mary were engaged to be married.

A Joseph was the town carpenter. He made…

B …wheels for carts…

A …doors for houses…

B …window frames…

A …ploughs for farms…

B …ladders for anyone who needed one…

A …and most of all, he made Mary happy.

B In those days, an engagement lasted for one year. At the end of that time would be the marriage. Mary was looking forward to that.

A But then something very wonderful happened. Mary had an unexpected visitor. It, or should I say he, was an…

B …angel. His name was Gabriel. Angels are messengers sent to earth by God.

A The meeting went like this…

B 'Mary,' said Gabriel, 'you are truly blessed! The Lord is with you.'

A Mary was frightened. She wasn't used to angels visiting her. She didn't understand what was happening.

B 'Don't be afraid,' said the angel. 'God is pleased with you.'

A And then came an even bigger surprise.

B 'You will have a son,' said the angel. 'His name will be Jesus.'

A One minute Mary was getting on with her daily work—the next minute an angel arrived and told her she was to have a baby.

B But the surprises hadn't finished, for Mary's baby was not to be just an ordinary baby.

A 'Your baby will be great,' continued the angel. 'He will be called the Son of God Most High. The Lord will make him king, just like his ancestor David.'

B Mary was even more puzzled. 'How can all this happen?' she asked. 'Joseph and I are not married yet.'

A 'This is God's doing,' said the angel. 'Your child will be called the holy Son of God.'

B And then the angel told her that her cousin Elizabeth, though she was very old, was also going to have a baby.

A The angel said something rather lovely to Mary…

B … 'Nothing is impossible for God!'

A I think Mary thought about that very often after the angel left her.

B Soon afterwards, Mary went and stayed with her cousin Elizabeth.

A They were both about to become mothers of very special babies.

B Elizabeth's son would be called John. We know him as John the Baptist. Mary's son would be called Jesus.

A It was while she was staying with Elizabeth that Mary made up a wonderful song. It starts like this:

B 'With all my heart I praise the Lord, and I am glad because of God my Saviour. He cares for me, his humble servant.' (Luke 1:46–48)

A Mary was very happy. After three months' stay with Elizabeth, she returned home to Nazareth and to Joseph.

B Just as she thought her baby would be born at home in Nazareth, something happened.

A Well, what was it? You can't just finish the story there!

B You'll just have to wait until next time to find out.

★ ★ ★ ★ ★ **PRAYER** ★ ★ ★ ★ ★

Dear God, we remember Mary saying, 'With all my heart I praise the Lord, and I am glad because of God my Saviour. He cares for me, his humble servant.' And we thank you for your care. Amen

Reproduced with permission from *Year-round assemblies* published by BRF 2003 (1 84101 328 5)

EXTENSION MATERIAL

HYMNS

69   Family of man
95   Rejoice in the Lord always
96   A still small voice
99   Love will never come to an end
100 I may speak
Any Christmas-related songs or carols

PSHCE LINKS

Key Stage 1
2a, 2c, 4d, 5g

Key Stage 2
1e, 2a, 2d, 2e, 2f, 4b, 4c, 4f, 5g

SUGGESTED ACTIVITIES

 Discuss the different feelings Mary must have had when she received the message from the angel.

 Discuss the different choices Mary had. What were the implications of a child being born out of wedlock when Mary was alive? Why was it such a 'big dilemma' then?

 Discuss how Mary's duties to Joseph might have conflicted with her duties to God. How was she placed in a difficult situation?

 Write down a conversation that might have happened between Mary and Joseph, when she told him what the angel said. How would he have reacted?

 Draw a picture of Mary. Around the outside, write all the things she might have been thinking when she knew she was going to have a special baby who was going to become a king.

 Write down all the jobs that you think Joseph would have done. In what ways was his job similar to a modern-day carpenter?

 Act out a conversation that Mary might have had with the angel. How did the angel convince Mary of what would happen?

 Act out a conversation between Elizabeth and Mary when Mary was staying with her. What different things do you think they might have talked about? What different reactions do you think they might have had?

BETHLEHEM AND BEYOND

Theme

The expectations we have of Christmas may be limited to getting rather than giving. Mary gave herself willingly to God, and became in return the mother of Jesus.

Aim

To round off the term's assemblies with the story of the birth of Jesus.

Bible reference

LUKE 2:1–21

Key verse

LUKE 2:11

This very day in King David's home town a Saviour was born for you. He is Christ the Lord.

Preparation

You will need a scroll for one of the Roman soldiers.

* *

CAST

Two narrators
Mary
Joseph
Roman soldiers
Two shepherds
Angels

STORY

SCENE ONE

Narrator 1   It was an ordinary day in Nazareth when the Roman soldiers came marching into town. 'Why are they here?' Mary whispered to Joseph. Then the centurion unrolled a scroll and started to read…

Soldiers march in, one with a scroll.

Narrator 2 'The Emperor Augustus has given orders. Everyone is to go to his or her family town to be registered. There will be no exceptions to this. You must all go. Old, young, fit and unfit. All must go by order of the Emperor. Long live the Emperor.' This was not good news for Mary…

Soldiers exit; Mary and Joseph set off.

Narrator 1 …because her baby was nearly due. Joseph was worried about Mary. You see, their family town was Bethlehem—the place where their ancestor David had been born. But it was eighty miles from Nazareth to Bethlehem. One thing was sure—they must travel slowly and others would be there before them.

were guarding their sheep. Let's get them to tell us in their own words what actually happened.

SCENE TWO

Mary and Joseph arrive and search for accommodation.

Narrator 2 It seemed to Joseph and Mary that everyone had got to Bethlehem before them. The town was crowded. Hundreds of people had returned to Bethlehem for the census. There was no room. All that could be found was a shelter used for animals. Mary's special son was born in a stable and laid in a manger. It was an extraordinary way for the Son of God to arrive on earth.

Mary and Joseph exit.

Narrator 1 Extraordinary things were taking place elsewhere. On the hillside above Bethlehem, some shepherds

SCENE THREE

Shepherds enter.

Shepherd 1 At first it seemed as though something, perhaps a wild animal, had frightened the sheep.

Shepherd 2 They started bleating and baaing…

Shepherd 1 …and then we saw the light. It wasn't like any light we'd seen before.

Shepherd 2 It was brighter than the brightest sunrise.

Shepherd 1 It was brighter than a flash of lightning.

Shepherd 2 It was terrifying. We just fell on the ground in a heap.

Shepherd 1 Then we heard this voice. It wasn't like any voice we'd heard before. It was sort of, well, angelic…

Shepherd 2 You great turnip, it *was* an angel! It was an angel with a message just for us.

Shepherd 1 There we were, all of a heap, hardly daring to look up, when the angel said…

Angel enters.

Shepherd 2 'Don't be afraid! I have good news for you, which will make everyone happy.'

Shepherd 1 Then he told us what the good news was.

Shepherd 2 He told us that a very special baby had just been born.

Shepherd 1 The angel said that the baby was in Bethlehem. We'd know who he was because he would be lying in a bed of hay.

Shepherd 2 Then there was a whole crowd of angels.

Enter more angels.

Shepherd 1 Hundreds…

Shepherd 2 …and hundreds…

Shepherd 1 …and hundreds of angels.

Shepherd 2 All-singing, all-dancing angels.

Shepherd 1 They lit up the whole sky.

Shepherd 2 I should think they could see the light and hear the singing in Bethlehem.

Angels exit; shepherds run on the spot.

Shepherd 1 So we ran as quick as we could down the hill into David's city.

Mary and Joseph enter. Shepherds kneel.

Shepherd 2 We found the baby. The angels were right—he *was* lying in hay.

Shepherd 1 Of course the angels were right— they wouldn't get the job if they didn't get things right!

Shepherd 2 Well, we told Mary and Joseph all about the angels. They were very surprised.

Narrator 1 The shepherds were so happy, they couldn't keep it to themselves. They sang their songs of praise through the streets, up the hill, and to the sheep! They were very happy shepherds!

Exit shepherds.

All (except angel) Long live Christ the Lord.

★ ★ ★ ★ ★ **PRAYER** ★ ★ ★ ★ ★

Lord of Christmas, thank you that we can join the shepherds in celebrating your birth in Bethlehem. We sing our songs of praise to you as we remember how you were born as a baby in a stable. Amen

Reproduced with permission from *Year-round assemblies* published by BRF 2003 (1 84101 328 5)

Extension material

HYMNS

116 Rise up, shepherd
117 I want to see your baby boy
120 As I went riding by
121 The Virgin Mary
123 Mary had a baby
Any Christmas-related songs or carols of your choosing

PSHCE LINKS

Key Stage 1
2a, 2b, 5c

Key Stage 2
2a, 2e, 2g, 4b

SUGGESTED ACTIVITIES

 Discuss the reaction of Mary and Joseph to the news that they had to travel to Bethlehem. How would they both have felt?

 Discuss how Mary and Joseph would have felt when the shepherds arrived at the stable.

 Write down some phrases that the shepherds might have said in their 'song of praise'. Can you put them together to make a poem or even a song?

 Draw a cartoon strip of the events leading up to the birth of Jesus. What different conversations and thought bubbles will you use?

 Act out a conversation between the shepherds who were addressed by the angel and some other shepherds who weren't there. What might be said? How would the other shepherds react?

 Act out how the donkey might be feeling as the three travellers made their way to Bethlehem. Can you develop a character for him?

 Research what life under Roman rule must have been like for Mary and Joseph. How would they have had to act? How does this differ from life in a democracy?

JESUS

INTRODUCTION TO THE SPRING TERM

The spring term begins with Jesus' childhood, which leads on to the preparation for his ministry through baptism and the temptation in the wilderness. As the term progresses, we follow Jesus as he chooses his disciples, goes to a wedding in Cana, teaches about God and heals many illnesses. Palm Sunday leads us to the last supper, trial, crucifixion and Easter Day.

As before, there are three ways of presenting the assemblies. The first of these is the use of two adult narrators, indicated by the letter (a). These assemblies generally come at the beginning and end of the term when there is less time to prepare class-led assemblies. The second type is the class-led assembly where one class, or group of children, is responsible for both the narration and the miming of the story. These assemblies are indicated by the letter (b). The third style of presentation, indicated by the letter (c), usually led by either one or two adult narrators, is interactive. Everyone joins in by making a certain defined response.

The 'Busy day' song provides continuity, as the verses summarize most of the events.

BUSY DAY

Every day was a busy day,
With chairs and tables, carts and beds,
Ploughs and windows, doors and sheds.
Every day was a busy day,
With hammer and nails, plane and saw,
With hammer and nails, plane and saw.

Every day was a busy day,
With rocks and sand, the wind and sun,
And the devil leading Jesus on.
Every day was a busy day,
In the deserted wilderness,
In the deserted wilderness.

Every day was a busy day,
With boats and sails, nets and fish,
'Now leave your boats, it is my wish.'
Every day was a busy day,
For the fishermen of Galilee,
For the fishermen of Galilee.

Every day was a busy day,
With teaching here, and healing there,
Things to do, no time for prayer.
Every day was a busy day
For Jesus from Nazareth,
For Jesus from Nazareth.

Every day was a busy day,
With shouts of praise, donkey trotting,
Palms all waving, soon forgotten.
Everyday was a busy day,
As Jesus rode into town,
As Jesus rode into town.

Every day was a busy day,
Friends meet together, come to dine,
Now pass the bread and drink the wine.
Every day was a busy day,
'Do this to remember me',
'Do this to remember me.'

Every day was a busy day,
Condemned to die, no pity shown,
Jesus God's son was there alone.
Every day was a busy day,
As darkness fell on Golgotha,
As darkness fell on Golgotha.

Every day was a busy day,
When Jesus became alive again,
And gently whispered Mary's name.
Every day was a busy day,
And nothing since has been the same,
And nothing since has been the same.

 Reproduced with permission from *Year-round assemblies* published by BRF 2003 (1 84101 328 5)

BUSY DAY

Music by Jo Dobbs
Lyrics by Brian Ogden

NazaReth

 Theme

Jesus is growing up and learning about his extended family. He also learns how his actions have an effect on others.

 Aim

To show how Jesus spent the first thirty years of his life preparing for the final three.

 Bible reference

LUKE 2:36–52; 3:1–20

 Key verse

LUKE 2:52

Jesus became wise, and he grew strong. God was pleased with him and so were the people.

 **Preparation**

No special preparation is needed.

★★

CAST

Two leaders / narrators (A and B)

STORY

A In our assemblies last term, we followed the life of David, the shepherd boy who became king.

B Just before Christmas, we thought about the birth of Jesus who was born in Bethlehem, the city of David.

A This term we shall be continuing the story of Jesus from where we left off.

B We shall follow it through some of the moments when Mary, Jesus' mother, was there.

A Jesus was born in Bethlehem but he grew up in the village of Nazareth.

B Jesus was Joseph and Mary's oldest son. Joseph was the village carpenter in Nazareth. The oldest son was always taught a trade by his father.

A So Jesus learned how to be a good carpenter.

B He made wheels for carts…

A …doors for houses…

B …window frames…

A …ploughs for farmers…

B …beds to sleep on…

A …and ladders for anyone who needed one. And he learned about people…

B …those who were poor and couldn't pay…

A …those were rich and wouldn't pay.

B But what about school? Did Jesus go to school?

A Yes, but it wasn't like this school. School was only for boys. They started when they were about six. They were taught in the synagogue and learned parts of the Jewish Scriptures by heart.

B What about the girls, then? Who taught them?

A The girls stayed at home and were taught by their mothers to cook and clean and to make and mend the family's clothes.

B So Jesus grew up at home in Nazareth learning to be a carpenter.

A That's right. But when Jesus was twelve, his parents took him to Jerusalem for the feast of the Passover. At twelve, a Jewish boy becomes a man. Any Jewish adult must go to Jerusalem for the Passover feast if they live within fifteen miles of the city.

B I should think Jesus was very excited about this. It must have been a bit like going to London for the first time.

A Yes, the city was crowded with travellers from many countries. Bright clothes, strange languages, shops full of things he would not have seen at home. It was very exciting.

B But all too soon it was time to go home— back to Nazareth. Mary and all the other women set off first.

A Joseph and the men came a little later. They walked faster than the women.

B Jesus was with the men?

A No, he wasn't.

B Jesus was with the women, taking care of Mary?

A No, he wasn't.

B You mean, when Joseph and Mary met up at the end of the first day's journey, Jesus was missing?

A Yes, he was. Joseph thought he was with Mary.

B And Mary thought he was with Joseph.

A Joseph and Mary hurried back to Jerusalem.

B They searched for three days but there was no sign of Jesus.

A They were very worried. And when parents are worried, they are usually cross.

B They found Jesus at last. He was in the temple.

A He was listening to all the wise men talking.

B When his mother saw him, she said, 'Son, why have you done this to us? Your father and I have been very worried.'

A That's the worried and cross bit. Well, it would have been if it was my mother!

B But Jesus reminded them that he was someone rather special.

A 'Didn't you know I would be in my Father's house?' he said.

B It was a reminder to Mary and Joseph that Jesus was the Son of God.

A This time they did go home together—back to Nazareth.

B But Mary never forgot what had happened and she kept on thinking about it.

A Meanwhile, not very far away, another boy was growing up.

B His name was John. John's mother was Elizabeth. Elizabeth and Mary were cousins.

A God had a very special job for John to do. He was to prepare the way for…

B …Jesus. John lived in the desert. Lots of people came to see him there.

A His message was this…

B Turn back to God and be baptized. Then your sins will be forgiven.

A The people wanted to know what they should do…

B …and John told them.

A If you have two coats, give one to someone who doesn't have any.

B If you have food, share it with someone else.

A He told the tax collectors not to steal.

B He told soldiers to be kind.

A John baptized many people who wanted to show that they were sorry and wanted to make a new start.

B One day, John had a surprise. And we'll tell you why next time.

A But I want to know what the surprise is now!

B You'll just have to wait!

★ ★ ★ ★ ★ **PRAYER** ★ ★ ★ ★ ★

Loving God, thank you for our families and for all who love us. Help us to play our part in family life by the things that we do and the things that we say. Amen

Reproduced with permission from *Year-round assemblies* published by BRF 2003 (1 84101 328 5)

EXTENSION MATERIAL

HYMNS

5   Somebody greater
22 Lord of the dance
27 A man for all the people
60 I listen and I listen

PSHCE LINKS

Key Stage 1
1a, 2a, 2c, 2e, 2f, 4a, 4d

Key Stage 2
1e, 2d, 4a, 4b, 4c

SUGGESTED ACTIVITIES

 Talk about what Jesus did at the synagogue. Did he act wrongly? Was it wrong of Jesus not to be with his parents? Was he being 'fair' to his parents? Discuss an occasion when you have had to choose between right and wrong.

 Discuss with a friend some of the things you might be prepared to share. Are they just possessions or are there other things? Does your discussion change the way you think about your possessions?

 Write down all the jobs you can think of that a carpenter did in Jesus' time. Draw pictures to go with them. How are they the same or different from today?

 Compare the differences between your average day and Jesus'. Which appeals more to you, and why?

 Act out how you think the conversation might have gone between Mary and Joseph when they discovered Jesus was missing, and when they found Jesus. What kinds of things would they have said?

 Research the ways John the Baptist prepared the way for Jesus. What did he do, and how did he live?

BAPTISM AND TEMPTATION

Theme

Jesus prepares himself for the work of God his father. He does not give in to temptation. Doing what is right is not always easy.

Aim

To teach about the baptism and testing of Jesus.

Bible reference

LUKE 3:21—4:13

Key verse

LUKE 3:22

A voice from heaven said, 'You are my own dear Son, and I am pleased with you.'

Preparation

A flat stone is needed.

* *

Six narrators
John the Baptist
Jesus
The devil
Crowd of people

STORY

Narrator 1 It was a really busy day for John. News had got round that he was baptizing people in the River Jordan. Great crowds went to see and hear him.

Crowd stand around John.

Narrator 2 'I baptize you with water so that the things you do wrong will be forgiven,' he told the people standing by. 'But someone more powerful is going to come. He will baptize you with the Holy Spirit and with fire.'

Narrator 3 Jesus' cousin, John the Baptist, was preparing the way for Jesus. Jesus was now thirty years old and had left his home in Nazareth.

Jesus enters.

Narrator 1 It was God's time for him to start his work. Jesus stood by the riverside with the other people waiting to be baptized.

John baptizes several people.

Reproduced with permission from *Year-round assemblies* published by BRF 2003 (1 84101 328 5)

Narrator 2 John couldn't believe that Jesus had come to him.

John and Jesus have a conversation.

Narrator 3 'I ought to be baptized by you,' said John. 'Why have you come to me?'
Narrator 1 'For now, this is how it should be,' said Jesus, 'because we must do all that God wants us to do.'
Narrator 2 John agreed and took Jesus down into the water of the River Jordan. John gently helped Jesus to duck under the surface of the water and then to stand again.

John leads Jesus into the water.

Narrator 3 As Jesus came out of the water, the Holy Spirit came to him looking like a dove.

John leads Jesus out of the water.

Narrator 1 Then a voice from heaven said, 'This is my own dear Son, and I am pleased with him.'

Narrator 4 After his baptism, Jesus left the River Jordan and went off by himself into the desert.

Exit John and the crowd. Jesus stands by himself.

Narrator 5 This area is sometimes called the wilderness. It was…
Narrator 6 …very hot by day…
Narrator 4 …and very cold at night.
Narrator 5 It was very dry and dusty.
Narrator 6 The rocks were bare and jagged.
Narrator 5 You could never be more alone than in the wilderness.
Narrator 6 Nothing grew there.
Narrator 4 Nothing lived there.
Narrator 5 No one came.
Narrator 6 Jesus was alone, thinking and praying about the days ahead.

Jesus kneels.

Narrator 4 He needed to be sure about the work God had for him to do.
Narrator 5 For forty days Jesus was in the desert. After all that time, he was hungry. It was then that…
Narrator 6 …the devil came to test him.

Enter the devil.

Narrator 4 'If you're God's Son, tell this stone to turn into bread,' said the devil.

Devil offers flat stone.

Narrator 5 Jesus said, 'Scripture says, "No one can live only on food."'
Narrator 6 The devil tried again. This time he took Jesus to a very high place.

Devil points.

Narrator 4	From there they could see all the nations on the earth.
Narrator 5	'I will give all this power and glory to you,' said the devil. 'Just worship me, and you can have it all.'
Narrator 6	Jesus answered, 'Scripture says, "Worship the Lord your God and serve only him!"'
Narrator 4	For the second time the devil had failed. He tried once more to test Jesus.
Narrator 5	The devil took Jesus to Jerusalem. They stood on the top of the temple.
Narrator 6	'If you are God's Son, jump off. After all, Scripture says…
Narrator 4	'God will tell his angels to take care of you. They will catch you in their arms, and you will not hurt your feet on the stones.'
Narrator 5	But Jesus knew Scripture better than the devil.
Narrator 6	'Scripture also says, "Don't try to test the Lord your God."'

Narrator 4	The devil tried many things, but Jesus did not fail the tests.

Devil exits.

Narrator 5	But what did it all mean?
Narrator 6	It was a very special time for Jesus. He was about to start the work he had come to earth to do.
Narrator 4	The devil showed him ways he could go about that work…
Narrator 5	…by giving people all they wanted, like turning stones into food…
Narrator 6	…by taking an easy way, not worrying much about right and wrong…
Narrator 4	…by tricking people into thinking he could jump off the temple and winning their interest to see what trick he would do next.
Narrator 5	But Jesus would have none of this. He knew that God's way was the only way.
Narrator 6	When he left the wilderness, he didn't go back to his home in Nazareth. He went instead to Capernaum by the side of the big lake.

Jesus exits.

Narrator 4	And it's here that we shall carry on our story next time.

★ ★ ★ ★ ★ **PRAYER** ★ ★ ★ ★ ★

Lord Jesus, you know how hard it is not to give in when we are tempted to do something wrong. Give us the strength to say 'no' when that is the right thing to say. Amen

Reproduced with permission from *Year-round assemblies* published by BRF 2003 (1 84101 328 5)

EXTENSION MATERIAL

HYMNS

22   Lord of the dance
25   When Jesus walked in Galilee
26   Jesus Christ is here
27   A man for all the people

PSHCE LINKS

Key Stage 1
1a, 1c, 2a, 2c, 4a, 4b, 5c, 5d

Key Stage 2
2d, 2e, 2f, 4a, 4b

SUGGESTED ACTIVITIES

 Discuss a topical situation where it would be hard to do 'the right thing'. What are the consequences of doing the right and the wrong thing in this example?

 Discuss the 'rules' Jesus was following in the wilderness. Would it have been easy? When are rules hard to follow?

 Write down some times when you have had to make a real choice between what you would have liked to do, and what you did. How did your actions affect others?

 Write down some of the characteristics you think Jesus would have had to possess to resist the devil and to do God's work.

 Act out a situation where someone does the wrong thing. How do these actions affect other people? Repeat the activity, but this time doing the right thing. Discuss what happens each time.

JESUS CHOOSES HIS FRIENDS

 Theme

Jesus chooses his disciples from a wide variety of people and shows that we all have something to offer, despite our differences.

 Aim

To show how Jesus chose his friends, even if some looked a bit unlikely!

 Bible reference

LUKE 5:1–11

 Key verse

LUKE 5:10

Jesus told Simon, 'Don't be afraid! From now on you will bring in people instead of fish.'

✂ **Preparation**

Cards or OHP acetates with the following responses are needed for the interactive story.

Lake Galilee: 'It's very big'
People: 'Crowds of people'
Fishermen: 'Have you caught anything?'
Row: 'In out, in out'

A list of the disciples' names on cards or OHP acetates is also needed.

Simon Peter
Andrew
James
John
Matthew
Thomas
Philip
James
Bartholomew
Nathanael
Thaddaeus
Judas Iscariot

★★★

CAST

Two leaders / narrators (A and B)

STORY

A After his time in the wilderness, Jesus made his home in the town of Capernaum. Capernaum is by the shore of LAKE GALILEE.

B LAKE GALILEE is thirteen miles long and eight miles wide.

A When Jesus lived on earth, there were a great many FISHERMEN who made their living from fishing in the lake.

B By now, the news about Jesus had spread everywhere…

A …and the PEOPLE came in large numbers to hear him.

B Pulled up on the shore, just out of the water, were two boats left by some FISHERMEN.

A The FISHERMEN were washing their nets in the lake.

B More and more PEOPLE were joining the crowd to listen to Jesus.

A Those at the back couldn't see.

B They couldn't hear very well, either.

A Jesus saw the boat on the edge of LAKE GALILEE and climbed into it.

B The boat belonged to Simon the FISHERMAN.

A Simon was a bit surprised to find Jesus the teacher sitting in his boat.

B 'Please ROW out a little bit from the shore,' said Jesus.

A Simon ROWED the boat out a short distance. The PEOPLE now had a better view and they could hear what Jesus was saying.

B I wonder what Simon thought about all this. Instead of washing his nets, he was sitting in his boat listening to Jesus.

A When Jesus finished speaking, Simon the FISHERMAN had another surprise.

B 'ROW your boat out to where the water is really deep,' said Jesus. 'If you drop your nets in LAKE GALILEE, you will catch some fish.'

A The PEOPLE had gone and only Simon heard what Jesus had to say.

B 'Master,' said Simon, 'we FISHERMEN worked hard all night and didn't catch a single fish. But if you want us to try again, we will.'

A Simon called the other FISHERMEN and they ROWED the boat out on to LAKE GALILEE.

B It was amazing. During the night, when the FISHERMEN usually fished, they had caught nothing.

A Now their nets were full to bursting with the bright silver fish.

B Simon and his crew couldn't manage alone. They signalled to the other FISHERMEN to come and help them.

A The others ROWED out and soon both boats were filled to overflowing with fish. They were flapping around everywhere.

B And so were the FISHERMEN!

A After a long hard ROW, they reached the shore. Simon was so amazed by what had happened that he knelt down in front of Jesus.

B James and John, the other FISHERMEN, were just as surprised.

A Then Jesus said something that surprised them even more.

77

Reproduced with permission from *Year-round assemblies* published by BRF 2003 (1 84101 328 5)

B 'From now on you will bring in PEOPLE instead of fish.'

A The FISHERMEN pulled their boats up on the shore and became the first friends and followers of Jesus.

Have four children come on carrying the names of Simon Peter, Andrew, James and John.

B And there were others…

Have eight children come on as the names are read out.

A There was Matthew, the tax collector who stopped taking money and started to follow Jesus.

B There was Thomas, who later on was to doubt that Jesus was alive again.

A There was Philip…

B …and James…

A …and Bartholomew…

B …and Nathanael…

A …and Thaddaeus…

B …and Judas Iscariot, who later betrayed Jesus.

A Jesus chose these ordinary men to be his friends.

B For the next three years, they followed Jesus wherever he went.

A Jesus taught them many things.

B It was these men who were the first to be with Jesus through good times and bad.

A It was because of the courage and faith of these men that we know about Jesus today.

B In our next story, Jesus takes his friends to a party.

A Oh good, I like parties!

★ ★ ★ ★ ★ **PRAYER** ★ ★ ★ ★ ★

Jesus, our friend and brother, help us to be wise in the choice of our friends, that we may be loyal to them and they to us. Amen

EXTENSION MATERIAL

HYMNS

23   Jesus, good above all other
25   When Jesus walked in Galilee
101   In the bustle of the city
103   I am planting my feet

PSHCE LINKS

Key Stage 1
2a, 2b, 5c, 5f

Key Stage 2
1a, 4b, 4c, 4f

SUGGESTED ACTIVITIES

 Discuss how the lives of the fishermen would have radically changed in one day. What were their lives like before Jesus chose them, and what were they like afterwards? Extend the discussion to include some of the other disciples.

 Discuss why Jesus chose 'ordinary' men to be his special friends. Why did he do that? Discuss the variety of jobs they all had before they followed Jesus.

 Write an account of the story as if you were Simon. How would you have felt as your boat was taken over? How would you have reacted to Jesus? What would you have thought of the amazing catch of fish?

 Act out a hot-seat situation with one person being Simon. What kind of questions would you want to ask him and how would he answer?

 Research the life of a fisherman in Jesus' times. How would it vary from today? What jobs were involved?

THE BEST-KEPT SECRET

 Theme

Jesus and Mary go to a wedding, and show how they care about other people through their actions.

 Aim

To show that even though Jesus is the Son of God, he cares about everyday problems.

 Bible reference

JOHN 2:1–12

 Key verse

JOHN 2:5

'Do whatever Jesus tells you to do.'

 Preparation

You will need a wedding invitation for Mary and a cup for one of the waiters.

★ ★

CAST

One leader / narrator
Mary
Jesus
Disciples
Two gossips
Waiters
Bride and groom
Wedding guests

STORY

The village of Cana was not far from Nazareth. In fact, most of the people who lived in Nazareth knew those who lived in Cana. They not only knew one another but they knew what was going on in each place. If a baby was born in one village they knew about it in the other. If an old person died in Nazareth, then they knew about it in Cana.

Most of all, if there was to be a wedding, then everybody knew about it. Jesus' mother, Mary, had a special invitation.

Mary pretends to look at invitation.

It's quite likely that she was related to the bride's family and had something to do with the arrangements for the wedding feast. The invitation to the wedding included Jesus, Mary's oldest son.

'Let him bring those new friends of his as well,' said the bride's family. 'It will be good to see them all there.'

Mary beckons small group on to stage and shows them the invitation.

There is no mention of Joseph on the invitation. It may well be that Joseph had died some years earlier. Because of this, Jesus stayed at home until he was thirty. He looked after his mother—and his younger brothers and sisters, until they could look after themselves.

In Palestine, a wedding was a very important occasion. The wedding took place late in the evening after a feast. It was a very happy time—that is to say, it was usually a very happy time. Sadly, at this wedding there was a bit of a problem.

It was the wine! At a wedding feast, wine was very important. It was a terrible disgrace if there was no wine, or if it had run out.

People would gossip about it on the streets.

Two gossips pretend to whisper to each other.

'Don't tell a soul, but they ran out of wine at their wedding!'

'Mean, that's what they are. Mean! He just wouldn't buy enough.'

The bride and bridegroom would never hear the end of it—they would never live it down.

It was Mary who noticed it first. She saw that the waiters were looking very worried. What could she do to avoid the disgrace? What could she do to stop the wedding being spoiled for the young couple? There must be something. Jesus. Jesus, her son, he might be able to help.

Worried-looking waiters mime, 'No more wine.'

Mary beckoned Jesus over to her. She took him to one side where the others couldn't hear.

Mary beckons Jesus.

'Jesus,' said Mary, 'they don't have any more wine. Please do something.'

Jesus understood how important it was. He almost certainly knew the couple and their parents.

Mary was sure that things would be all right now. She spoke to the waiters.

Mary speaks to waiters.

'Whatever Jesus tells you to do, make sure you do it,' she said.

Standing just outside the house were six stone water jars. They held the water that was used by people to wash their feet after a journey and their hands before a meal. Each jar held about one hundred litres of water.

'Fill these jars right to the top with water,' Jesus told the waiters.

 Reproduced with permission from *Year-round assemblies* published by BRF 2003 (1 84101 328 5)

Jesus tells waiters to fill the stone jars.

It took some time but at last every jar was full. The waiters looked at Jesus. Whatever was he going to tell them to do now?

'Take some of the water from one of the jars and take it to the head waiter,' said Jesus.

One waiter takes a cup to head waiter, who tries the wine.

Carefully a cup of wine was taken from one of the jars to the head waiter. He didn't know where it had come from. He lifted the cup to his lips. This was good. This was very good. This wine tasted better than the wine they had served at the beginning of the feast. It was most unusual.

The head waiter went over to the bridegroom.

Head waiter goes over to the bridegroom.

'Usually,' he said, 'we serve the best wine first. Then, when the guests have had that, they don't notice the cheaper wine. You've done it the other way round. You've kept the best until last!'

It was the best-kept secret at the wedding.

After the feast, the actual marriage ceremony took place. The bride was beautiful. The groom was handsome and the wine was delicious. It was a very happy wedding. After the wedding, the young couple were taken to their new home by their friends and relations.

Crowd conduct couple to their home.

Jesus, his mother and his friends left Cana and went back to Capernaum, where he stayed for a few days.

Jesus, Mary and friends leave.

★ ★ ★ ★ ★ **PRAYER** ★ ★ ★ ★ ★

Father God, you made us to enjoy quiet times and party times. Help us at all times to be aware of the needs of others. Amen

Reproduced with permission from *Year-round assemblies* published by BRF 2003 (1 84101 328 5)

EXTENSION MATERIAL

HYMNS

24 Go, tell it on the mountain
26 Jesus Christ is here
27 A man for all the people
29 From the darkness came light

PSHCE LINKS

Key Stage 1
2a, 2f, 4b, 4c, 4d, 5c

Key Stage 2
2e, 2i, 4b, 4c, 4e, 4f

SUGGESTED ACTIVITIES

 Discuss the qualities of Mary in the story. What attributes do you think she shows and why do you think this?

 Discuss whether Mary did the right thing. Was she helping out or was she interfering? What do you think?

 Write about the wedding as if you were one of the guests. How would you have felt? What would you have seen? What might you have said?

 Act out a conversation between two of the waiters as they realize the wine is running low. What would they have said? How would they have felt? Who was going to tell the head waiter?

 Act out a hot-seat situation with Mary in the hot seat. What might you want to ask her?

 Research a modern Jewish wedding. How has the ceremony changed, and how has it stayed the same since Jesus' time?

HOME AND AWAY

 Theme

Jesus was no longer allowed to teach in the synagogues, and he began to challenge the religious leaders. Jesus, for the right reasons, was very sure of himself.

 Aim

To show the reason that Jesus came to earth.

 Bible reference

LUKE 4:14–44

 Key verse

LUKE 4:18

The Lord's Spirit has come to me, because he has chosen me to tell the good news to the poor.

 Preparation

Prepare a scroll similar to that used in a synagogue.

CAST

Two leaders / narrators (A and B)

STORY

A Jesus had been baptized by John.

B He had been tempted by the devil.

A He had chosen some friends to be with him and…

B …they had all been to a wedding party.

A But the real work Jesus had to do was to teach people about God and about his kingdom.

B Every Sabbath, the day we call Saturday, all Jewish people went to the synagogue.

A The synagogue is the Jewish place of worship, just as the Christian place of worship is the church.

B The Jewish law says that where there are ten families there must be a synagogue. So in every village and town there was a synagogue.

A There were three parts to the service in a synagogue.

B There was the part where prayers were said.

A There was the reading from holy Scriptures. For Jewish people, this is the part of the Bible we know as the Old Testament.

B And there was the teaching part, where a priest or wise person might be asked to speak.

A News about Jesus spread everywhere. He was a popular speaker.

B He spoke in the synagogues of many of the towns and villages in Galilee.

A One day, Jesus went back to Nazareth. Perhaps he went to see his mother, Mary.

B On the Sabbath day, Jesus went as usual to the synagogue.

A He was given the scroll containing the book of Isaiah to read, and this is what he read.

Show prepared scroll.

B 'The Lord's Spirit has come to me, because he has chosen me to tell the good news to the poor. The Lord has sent me to announce freedom for prisoners, to give sight to the blind, to free everyone who suffers, and to say, "This is the year the Lord has chosen."'

A Jesus handed back the scroll and sat down. It was the custom for the teacher to sit to speak to the people.

B Everyone in the synagogue knew Jesus. He might have made a door or ladder for them when he was their carpenter.

A Everyone knew Jesus' mother, Mary. They were friends with his brothers and sisters.

B It was then that Jesus said something which astonished and amazed everyone listening…

A 'What you have just heard me read has come true today.'

B And then, in the middle of the synagogue

service, everyone started to talk at once.

A 'But this is Joseph's son. Who does he think he is?'

B 'I wonder what poor Mary thinks of all this.'

A 'I always thought he was a strange boy.'

B 'How dare he come saying such things to us!'

A Jesus said to them, 'No prophets are liked by the people of their own home town.'

B But the people became really angry. They didn't want to hear the message that Jesus brought.

A Jesus was dragged out of the synagogue and taken to the edge of a cliff on the outskirts of the town.

B The people of Nazareth wanted to throw him over the cliff. The people with whom he had grown up wanted to kill him.

A But Jesus had not completed his work. He slipped through the crowd and went back to Capernaum.

B There, once again, he taught the people on the Sabbath. He spoke with great power and understanding. The people loved to hear him.

A In the middle of one service, there was a violent interruption.

  Reproduced with permission from *Year-round assemblies* published by BRF 2003 (1 84101 328 5)

B The people in the synagogue stood there with mouths wide open. Some of them edged away from the man who was mentally ill.

A What would Jesus do now? Could he, would he, do anything to help?

B Jesus went over to the man and spoke to him.

A Suddenly the place was quiet. Everyone watched as the man fell to the floor and lay there quietly. Jesus had made him well.

B The people were astonished.

A 'What kind of teaching is this?'

B 'He has the power to make people well.'

A 'I wouldn't have believed it if I hadn't seen it with my own eyes.'

B And the news about Jesus spread further and further.

B In the synagogue was a man who was mentally ill. To everyone's surprise, he suddenly shouted out…

A 'Hey, Jesus of Nazareth, what do you want with us? I know who you are! You are God's Holy One.'

★ ★ ★ ★ ★ **PRAYER** ★ ★ ★ ★ ★

Holy God, help us to know the truth when we hear it and, having heard it, to act on it. Amen

EXTENSION MATERIAL

HYMNS

21   Come and praise the Lord our King
22   Lord of the dance
24   Go, tell it on the mountain
28   Judas and Mary

PSHCE LINKS

Key Stage 1
2a, 2b, 2d, 2f, 4b, 4c, 5c

Key Stage 2
2b, 2e, 2i, 4b, 4e

SUGGESTED ACTIVITIES

 Discuss how Jesus acted. Did he do the right thing? How would he have felt at the people's reactions?

 Discuss how Mary must have felt. What would she have thought about what Jesus did?

 Discuss how Jesus would have felt. As these people all knew him, would it have been a surprise to him that they reacted as strongly as they did?

 Write about what happened as if you were actually in the synagogue when Jesus spoke. How would you react? What might you think?

 Act out a conversation between two people who saw what Jesus did in the synagogue. One person might agree; one might disagree. What would they say?

 Research what happens in a modern Jewish synagogue service. Examine the difference between the Orthodox and Liberal Jews. Compare your findings with what you know of Jesus' time.

SOW WHAT?

 Theme

Jesus uses stories to teach about the kingdom of God. He uses the fact that people are different from each other to illustrate his teaching.

 Aim

To show how Jesus used stories to teach people about God.

 Bible reference

LUKE 8:4–15

 Key verse

LUKE 8:15

Those seeds that fell on good ground are the people who listen to the message and keep it in good and honest hearts.

 Preparation

Two cards or OHP slides as follows, with responses for the interactive storytelling (shown by capitals in the text).

'Yes, they would.'
'Yes, there are people like that!'

****

CAST

A narrator
A reader for the words in italics

STORY

Winnie the Pooh, Bob the Builder and Harry Potter are all favourite stories. All of you could add your favourite story to that list. Everyone loves a good story. A good story makes us think. We want to know if the hero gets out of trouble. We want to know if the baddie gets into trouble! If we are listening to a story, we become the illustrator, because we can see the story in our imagination. Stories are fun but stories can also teach us a lot.

Jesus knew that people liked to listen to stories. Jesus often used stories to teach about God. He told the story about a man being mugged who was helped by a foreigner—we call that the story of the good Samaritan. He told a story about a shepherd who had to search for a sheep that went missing—we call that the story of the lost sheep.

A good story makes us want to be involved. Jesus knew that stories can make us think about what we do.

Once upon a time, a huge crowd had come to hear Jesus speak. There were fishermen and farmers, shopkeepers and shepherds, old people and children. They were sitting on the ground waiting for Jesus to start, hoping that he would tell them a good story.

'I wonder what he'll tell us today,' said a fisherman.

'It might be about those builders again,' said an elderly man. 'The one who built his house on sand and the other who built on a rock. That was a good story.'

'He might tell the one about the money lender who didn't want his money back,' said a shop-keeper. 'I wish I knew a money lender like that!'

Jesus started his story. Everyone was silent.

'One day, a farmer went out to scatter his seed.'

In those days, farmers held a bag of seed from which they took handfuls. The seeds were then scattered.

'While the farmer was doing it, some of the seeds fell on the path.'

YES, THEY WOULD.

Many people walked along the paths. The paths were made of hard mud and stones. The seeds would never take root.

'The birds swooped down and ate the seeds lying on the mud.'

YES, THEY WOULD.

'Other seed fell on rocky ground where the soil was very thin. The little plants grew quickly, but just as quickly they died, because there was no water.'

YES, THEY WOULD.

'The farmer scattered more seed, which fell in the middle of thorns and other weeds. When the thorns and the other weeds grew up, they choked the growing seeds.'

YES, THEY WOULD.

'Most of the seeds fell into good ground—the ground that the farmer had ploughed. Those seeds grew well and produced lots of healthy plants.'

YES, THEY WOULD.

Everyone enjoyed the story that Jesus told. They had all scattered seeds. They had seen what happened if the seeds fell on a path, or on stony ground or among weeds. They understood that for seed to grow properly it must fall into good ground.

It didn't look as though Jesus was going to tell any more stories that day, and the crowd went away. But the friends of Jesus, his disciples, were

 Reproduced with permission from *Year-round assemblies* published by BRF 2003 (1 84101 328 5)

puzzled. They wanted to know what the story meant. So Jesus took them on one side and answered them.

'This is what the story means. The seed is God's message. The seeds that fell on the hard path and never took root are people who won't even begin to listen to God's message.'

YES, THERE ARE PEOPLE LIKE THAT!

'The seeds that fell on rocky ground are people who hear God's message and know that it is right. But they only believe for a short time. When things are hard, they give up.'

YES, THERE ARE PEOPLE LIKE THAT!

'The seeds that fell in between the thorns and weeds are also people who hear God's message. For them, making lots of money and having a good time is what really matters. They are so busy with these things that they soon give up.'

YES, THERE ARE PEOPLE LIKE THAT!

'The seeds that fell on the good ground are people who listen to God's message. They think about what God means and they go out and do what God wants. And they don't give up—they keep at it.'

YES, THERE ARE PEOPLE LIKE THAT!

Jesus knew that telling stories was a very good way of teaching. Jesus told lots of stories and we can read them all in the Bible.

★ ★ ★ ★ ★ **PRAYER** ★ ★ ★ ★ ★

Jesus, storyteller supreme, help us to understand your stories and also to learn from them. Amen

EXTENSION MATERIAL

HYMNS

42   Travel on
47   One more step
53   Peace, perfect peace
134   I planted a seed

PSHCE LINKS

Key Stage 1
1b, 2a, 2c, 2g, 4b, 4c

Key Stage 2
1a, 2e, 4a, 4b, 4f

SUGGESTED ACTIVITIES

 Discuss the different types of people that Jesus refers to. How else could they be represented (other than the thorns / path analogy)?

 Discuss what type of person you think you might be, with regard to hearing a story and acting on it afterwards. Is that the type of person you want to be? How might you change?

 Write a short extract, retelling the story as if you were one of the disciples who didn't understand the meaning of the story. Does this help you to understand the story any better?

 Draw a comic strip showing the different types of ground that the seeds fell on to and what happened to each. Write next to each picture what type of person it represents.

 Write a prayer based on this parable, asking God to help you to be more like the seed that fell on good ground, and to show you ways to fulfil that desire.

 Act out a conversation with a friend (or some friends) as if you had just heard the story and you were trying to make sense of it. What ideas do you come up with?

IN JERUSALEM

✿ Theme
Jesus enters Jerusalem. He shows the crowds how the temple should be respected. Respect for property and for people is very important.

◎ Aim
To show Jesus' courage.

📖 Bible references
PALM SUNDAY: LUKE 19:28–40

IN THE TEMPLE: MATTHEW 21:12–17

🔑 Key verse
LUKE 19:38

Blessed is the king who comes in the name of the Lord!

✂ Preparation
You will need to rehearse two separate mimes.

The first mime relates to Palm Sunday. An effective way of showing the ride into Jerusalem is to have a row of children facing away from the assembly. They all begin by looking to the left, and then slowly move their heads to the right to indicate someone moving past them. These children should join in the triumphal shouts, 'Blessed is the king who comes in the name of the Lord!' and 'Peace in heaven and glory to God!' They might wave cardboard branches.

The second mime relates to the incident in the temple and can be performed with more or less detail. The money changers and dove sellers could shout to advertise their particular interests.

★★★★★★★★★★★★★★★★★★★★★★★★★★★★★★★★★★★★

CAST
Six narrators

STORY

Narrator 1	After three years of teaching and healing, Jesus started his last journey.
Narrator 2	Jesus knew that he had angered the religious leaders by what he had taught.
Narrator 3	He had angered them by claiming to be the Son of God.
Narrator 1	Jesus knew that they wanted to kill him, but on the day we call Palm Sunday…
Narrator 2	…he rode into the city of Jerusalem in such a way that everyone knew he was there. It was a very brave thing to do.

93

Narrator 3   But let's start the story at the beginning.

Narrator 1   'Go to the next village,' said Jesus to two of his friends. 'There you will find a young donkey. Untie the donkey and bring it here.'

Narrator 2   'If anyone asks what you are doing, just say, "The Lord needs it."'

Narrator 3   Jesus' two friends did what he asked and led the donkey back to Jesus.

Narrator 1   They put their cloaks on the donkey and helped Jesus to get on.

Narrator 2   Jesus turned the donkey's head towards the city.

The first mime starts here.

Narrator 3   As he rode along, the crowds gathered. Soon there were hundreds of people waving and cheering.

Narrator 1   'Blessed is the king who comes in the name of the Lord!'

Narrator 2   'Peace in heaven and glory to God!'

Narrator 3   Some of the religious leaders in the crowd spoke to Jesus.

Narrator 1   'Teacher, make your friends stop shouting!'

Narrator 2   'If they keep quiet, these stones will start shouting,' said Jesus.

Narrator 3   The ride into Jerusalem was a way of showing the people who Jesus was.

Narrator 1   In those days, the donkey was a noble animal. When a king entered a city in peace, he rode on a donkey.

The first mime ends here.

Narrator 2   What Jesus was doing was showing everyone that he came as a king of love and peace.

Narrator 3   But as we know, Jesus had enemies. He was about to do something that would make his enemies even more angry.

Narrator 4   The next part of our story takes place in the temple in Jerusalem.

Narrator 5 The temple was the most important place of worship and, like Christian cathedrals, was visited by hundreds of people.

Narrator 6 There were several parts of the temple. On the outside was the Court of the Gentiles. Anyone could go there…

Narrator 4 …and they did! It was crowded with people. They had come from miles around for one of the most important festivals—the Passover feast. There were pilgrims from all over the world.

The second mime starts here.

Narrator 5 The Court of the Gentiles was full of street traders—the money changers and the people who sold doves.

Narrator 6 At the time of the Passover festival, everyone had to pay a temple tax. But you couldn't pay it in ordinary money.

Narrator 4 You had to change your ordinary money into special money to pay your tax. And that's where the money changers came in.

Narrator 5 They charged you for changing your money!

Narrator 6 As well as the money changers, there were people who sold the doves that would be offered to God. The price of doves inside the temple was much higher than outside.

Narrator 4 Jesus went into the Court of the Gentiles and saw what was going on. He saw the money changers and dove sellers.

Narrator 5 The temple had been built for prayer and worship. It made Jesus both sad and angry to see what was happening.

Narrator 6 Jesus stormed over to the money changers and…

Narrator 4 …turned over their tables, scattering their money everywhere.

Narrator 5 Jesus marched over to the dove sellers and…

Narrator 6 …turned over their tables, releasing the doves into the air.

Narrator 4 Jesus said, 'The Scriptures say, "My house should be called a place of worship." But you have turned it into a place where robbers hide.'

The second mime ends here.

Narrator 5 When Jesus rode into Jerusalem, it was the beginning of the week that Christians call Holy Week— the week that would include Good Friday and Easter Day.

★ ★ ★ ★ ★ **PRAYER** ★ ★ ★ ★ ★

Eternal God, creator of the universe, help us to remember who you are and what you have done for us. Help us to praise you in our lives. Amen

EXTENSION MATERIAL

HYMNS

21 Come and praise the Lord our King
22 Lord of the dance
128 Trotting, trotting
132 When from the sky

PSHCE LINKS

Key Stage 1
1a, 1b, 2a, 2b, 2i, 4a, 4b, 5c

Key Stage 2
1a, 2b, 4a, 4b

SUGGESTED ACTIVITIES

 Discuss the actions of Jesus. Debate how his behaviour could be seen as courageous or controversial.

 Debate what Jesus did. Was he right to act as he did? Did he have any other choices?

 Write an account of what happened as if you were a bystander when Jesus rode into Jerusalem on the donkey.

 Write a newspaper report describing what Jesus did in the temple. You could also make up a few interviews with witnesses.

 Draw the scene as you imagine it when Jesus rode into Jerusalem, or when he went into the temple.

 Act out the temple scene. What types of things would have been said? How would people have reacted to the disturbance?

A SECRET SIGN

 Theme

Jesus shares a special meal with his friends, and uses bread and wine to convey a lasting message. Sharing with friends deepens friendship.

 Aim

To show how Jesus left Christians a very special way to remember him.

 Bible reference

LUKE 22:7–20; PSALM 136:1–9

> **Key verses**
>
> LUKE 22:19–20
>
> *'This is my body, which is given for you. Eat this as a way of remembering me! … This is my blood. It is poured out for you, and with it God makes his new agreement.'*

✂ **Preparation**

Assemble the following four items to put on a table when describing the preparations for the Passover feast:

- A bowl of salt water
- A collection of bitter herbs
- The charosheth paste
- Four cups of wine

If you have access to a chalice and paten from a local church, then these too can be shown.

On card or an OHP acetate, print the chorus line from Psalm 136: 'His love never fails'.

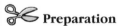

CAST

Two leaders / narrators (A and B)

STORY

A Jesus first went to Jerusalem for the feast of Passover at the age of twelve.

B That was when his parents had to search for him and found him at last in the temple.

A But this visit to Jerusalem, about twenty years later, was very different. Jesus had been teaching people about the kingdom of God.

B He had made many enemies among the religious leaders. He knew he was about to die.

A One last thing that Jesus wanted to do more than any other was to celebrate the Passover meal with his friends.

B The Passover celebrates what happened when the Israelites left Egypt, hundreds of years before Jesus was born.

A   It is a story from the Old Testament, the first part of the Christian Bible. It was a time when the Israelites were slaves in Egypt.

B   God told Moses to lead his people out of Egypt. The Egyptians took a lot of persuading to allow it to happen.

A   The Israelites were told to mark their houses so that the angel of God would pass over them.

B   The Passover feast has been celebrated ever since. For Jesus and his friends it was to be a very special time.

A   But they needed somewhere to meet. It would have to be quite a large room. Jerusalem was crowded. Everyone was looking for a place where they could celebrate the Passover. Jesus told two of his closest friends, Peter and John, to go and get ready the Passover meal.

B   'But where do you want us to prepare it?' they asked.

A   It was then that Jesus explained the secret sign to them.

B   'As you go into the city, you will meet a man carrying a jar of water. Follow him into the house and say to the owner, "Our teacher wants to know where he can eat the Passover meal with his disciples." The owner will take you upstairs and show you a large room ready for you to use.'

A   Following a man carrying a jar of water may not sound much like a secret sign to us. But it would have been to Peter and John.

B   Carrying water was a woman's job. A man carrying water would really have stuck out in a crowd.

A   Peter and John went into the crowded city and saw the man with the water jar. They followed him through the busy streets to a house.

B   Houses often had two rooms, one built on top of the other. The upper room was reached by outside stairs.

A   Peter and John were busy getting everything ready on that Thursday.

B   During the morning they prepared unleavened bread. Unleavened bread has no yeast in it.

A   It was a reminder that the Israelites had no time to wait for their bread to rise before they left Egypt.

B   They had put out a bowl of salt water…

A   …as a reminder of tears they had cried as slaves.

B   There was a collection of bitter herbs…

A   …as a reminder of the bitterness of slavery.

B   They had made a special paste called the Charosheth…

A   …as a reminder of the clay they had used when forced to make bricks for the Egyptians.

B   They set out four cups of wine…

A   …to remind them of the four promises that God made.

B   Just after six o'clock, Jesus and his other friends arrived ready to start the feast.

A   Jesus did two very special things that evening. First of all, he celebrated the traditional Passover feast with his friends.

B   The second very special thing that Jesus did was to share bread and some wine with his friends.

A   As they sat around the table, Jesus picked up a piece of bread. He said 'thank you' to God for it and broke it into small pieces.

B   'This is my body,' said Jesus, 'which is given for you. Eat this as a way of remembering me.'

A   Each of his friends took a small piece of bread and ate it.

B   After the meal had ended, Jesus took a cup of wine. He said 'thank you' to God for it and handed it to his friends.

A   'This is my blood,' said Jesus. 'It is poured out for you.'

B   Each of his friends took a sip of wine.

A   Ever since, for more than two thousand years, Christians have shared bread and wine together. Sometimes this is called 'The Lord's Supper', sometimes 'The Eucharist', or 'Holy Communion' or 'Mass'. These are different names for the same service.

B   At the end of the meal, Jesus and his friends sang a hymn. It was Psalm 136, which was always sung at the end of a Passover meal.

A   We are going to read the first nine verses of the psalm. Each verse has a chorus line which is, 'God's love never fails'. Please join in the chorus.

B   Praise the Lord! He is good.
God's love never fails.

A   Praise the God of all gods.
God's love never fails.

B   Praise the Lord of lords.
God's love never fails.

A   Only God works great miracles.
God's love never fails..

B   With wisdom he made the sky.
God's love never fails.

A   The Lord stretched the earth over the ocean.
God's love never fails.

B   He made the bright lights in the sky.
God's love never fails.

A   He lets the sun rule each day.
God's love never fails.

B   He lets the moon and the stars rule each night.
God's love never fails.

A   After they sang this hymn, Jesus and his friends went out into the night. He led them to the Mount of Olives.

★ ★ ★ ★ ★ **PRAYER** ★ ★ ★ ★ ★

Be with us in our work and play—
   God, whose love never fails.
Be with us at times of temptation—
   God, whose love never fails.
Be with us when we are frightened of what the day will bring—
   God, whose love never fails.
Be with us when human friendship fails—
   God, whose love never fails.
Amen

Reproduced with permission from *Year-round assemblies* published by BRF 2003 (1 84101 328 5)

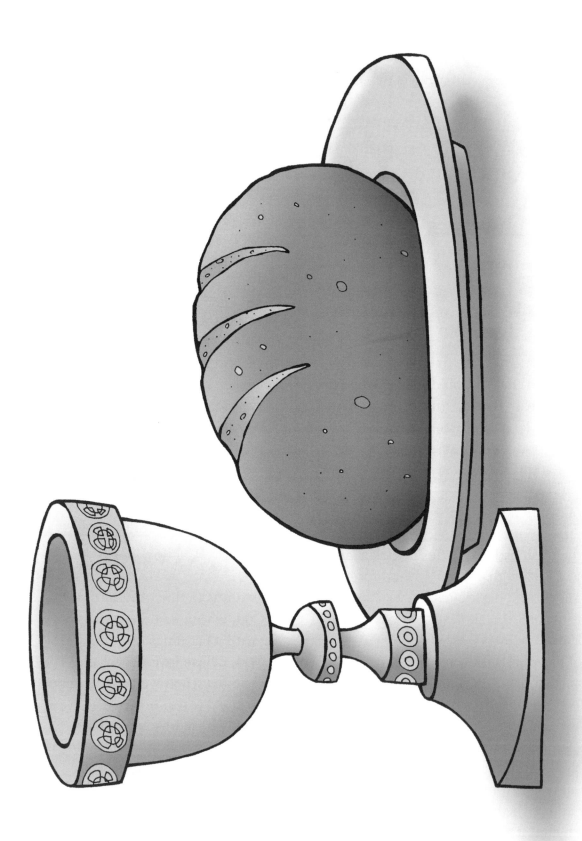

EXTENSION MATERIAL

HYMNS

25 When Jesus walked in Galilee
26 Jesus Christ is here
27 A man for all the people
29 From the darkness came light

PSHCE LINKS

Key Stage 1
2a, 4b, 4c, 4d, 5c

Key Stage 2
1a, 4b, 4c, 4f

SUGGESTED ACTIVITIES

 Discuss the use of signs in today's society. How many different signs can you recognize? How many are related to marketing and how many are indicative of a society or group of people?

 Discuss whether there are jobs today that are viewed as 'women's work'? Debate attitudes towards chores, and make a list of jobs that are gender-specific and jobs that are not.

 Draw the different constituent parts of the Passover meal. Can you remember what the significance of each one is? Do people still celebrate the Passover today?

 Write a diary account of the last supper as if you were one of the disciples. How would you have felt? What would you have thought? Did Jesus' words seem odd?

 With a group of friends, try to compose a tune to go with Psalm 136. Can you perform it to the rest of your class?

 Have a go at writing a prayer based around Psalm 136.

GOOD FRIDAY?

Theme

Jesus is arrested and crucified. He follows God's will, even though it leads to death. Doing the right thing is not always the easiest way.

Aim

To show how Jesus followed God's plan to the end.

Bible reference

LUKE 22:54—23:56

Key verse

LUKE 23:47

'Jesus must really have been a good man!'

Preparation

Two parts of the story can be mimed. The first is the scene in the garden of Gethsemane. The second scene is a part of the trial.

★★★

CAST

Six narrators
Jesus
Disciples
Temple police
Pilate
Religious leaders
Roman soldiers

STORY

Narrator 1   Our last assembly ended with Jesus and his friends walking through the night to the Mount of Olives.

A group walks to the centre of the area and kneels down.

Narrator 2   The Mount of Olives is a hill overlooking the city of Jerusalem. On the lower slopes of the hill is the garden of Gethsemane. It was a quiet place and Jesus often went there to pray.

Silence is kept for a short time, after which the first mime begins.

Narrator 3 But on this night the silence was shattered when the temple police and some of the religious leaders burst into the garden.

A group of temple police and religious leaders enters.

Narrator 1 At first, Jesus' friends stayed with him. But when Jesus was arrested and led away, his friends ran off into the darkness of the garden.

Jesus is arrested and led away. His friends run off and hide. End of mime.

Narrator 2 Jesus was taken to the house of the high priest. At daybreak, Jesus was brought before the Sanhedrin, the religious court.

Narrator 3 'Tell us, are you the Son of God?' they asked him.

Narrator 1 'If I said so, you wouldn't believe me,' answered Jesus. 'From now on, the Son of Man will be seated at the right side of God All-Powerful.'

Narrator 2 This made the religious leaders really angry. The high priest shouted, 'This man claims to be God! You have heard what he said. What do you think?'

Narrator 3 The Council answered, 'He is guilty and deserves to die.'

Narrator 1 But there was a problem as far as the religious leaders were concerned. They could not put a man to death. The sentence of death could only be given by the Roman governor and carried out by Roman soldiers.

Narrator 4 So Jesus had to be taken to Pontius Pilate, the Roman governor.

Second mime starts: Pilate faces the crowd, who have their backs to the audience.

Narrator 5 'We caught this man trying to get our people to riot and stop paying taxes to the Emperor,' said the religious leaders. 'He also claims to be the Messiah, our long-awaited king.'

Narrator 6 Pilate questioned Jesus and after a moment spoke again to the chief priest and the crowd. 'I don't find him guilty of anything,' he said. 'I will have him beaten and set free.'

Narrator 4 But the religious leaders had stirred up the crowd. The same people who cheered Jesus as he rode into the city a week before now shouted for his death.

The crowd shout, 'Kill him' and wave their fists.

Narrator 5 Finally, Pilate gave in and handed Jesus over to the soldiers.

The soldiers march off with Jesus. End of mime.

Reproduced with permission from *Year-round assemblies* published by BRF 2003 (1 84101 328 5)

Narrator 6 By this time, Jesus was weak. He had had no sleep. He had been badly treated by the soldiers. He was expected to carry a heavy part of his cross through the streets. Soon he stumbled.

Narrator 4 Standing in the crowd, watching this awful procession, was a man called Simon. He must have been tall and strong. The Roman soldiers guarding Jesus stopped and pulled Simon out of the crowd. They made him carry the cross-piece for Jesus.

Narrator 5 At last they reached the place called Golgotha. It was here that the crosses would stand. As well as Jesus, there were two robbers sentenced to death.

Narrator 6 Jesus was put on the cross. As this was happening, Jesus said, 'Father, forgive these people. They don't know what they're doing.'

Narrator 4 As Jesus hung on the cross, a huge crowd gathered. The religious leaders shouted insults. 'He saved others. Now he should save himself, if he really is God's chosen Messiah.'

Narrator 5 The Roman soldiers joined in, 'If you are the king of the Jews, save yourself.'

Narrator 6 In the crowd, there were many of Jesus' friends. Mary, his mother, was also there and John, his favourite disciple.

Narrator 4 Jesus saw Mary and John. From the cross he said to Mary, 'This man is now your son.' To John he said, 'She is now your mother.'

Narrator 5 The Bible tells us that at midday the sky turned dark and stayed that way until three o'clock in the afternoon.

Narrator 6 At that time, Jesus gave a great

shout, 'It is finished.' His work was done. As he died, the earth shook. All the people standing there felt the earthquake and were terrified.

Narrator 4 In charge of the Roman soldiers was a centurion. When he saw what had happened, he said these words, 'This man really was God's Son.'

Narrator 5 There was now nothing to watch and the crowds went home. As they left, a man called Joseph took Jesus' body from the cross. He wrapped it in fine cloth and carried it to a tomb, like a cave, cut out of the rock.

Narrator 6 It was late on Good Friday. Jesus was dead. It must have seemed like the end of everything for Jesus' friends—but Good Friday was soon to be followed by Easter Day.

★ ★ ★ ★ ★ **PRAYER** ★ ★ ★ ★ ★

Jesus, you never faltered in knowing what you must do. Help us in hard times to be strong, to do what must be done. Amen

EXTENSION MATERIAL

HYMNS

28   Judas and Mary
129 Jesus in the garden
130 All in an Easter garden
131 Now the green blade rises

PSHCE LINKS

Key Stage 1
1a, 1b, 2a, 2b, 4b, 4c, 4d

Key Stage 2
1a, 2a, 2b, 2c, 4b, 4c, 4f

SUGGESTED ACTIVITIES

 Discuss the actions of the religious leaders. What basis did they have for trying to kill Jesus?

 Discuss what it must have felt like to be one of the disciples, and to know what was happening to Jesus. What emotions would they have felt? Can you support each feeling with an extract from the story?

 Discuss how helpless Pilate might have felt. He could not find a reason for killing Jesus but he was being pressurized by the Jewish leaders and the crowd. What might he have thought and said?

 Draw a comic strip of the events in the assembly. Which speech and thought bubbles will you add? How will you show the expressions on people's faces?

 Write a newspaper article about the arrest of Jesus. You may decide to include a drawing and some 'interviews' with members of the crowd.

 Research the Roman laws of the time, and how they differed from the Jewish laws.

ALIVE AGAIN!

 Theme

Jesus reappears to his special friends. Mary believes, while Thomas demands evidence. Easter is about new life.

 Aim

To consider the basis of Christian faith—that Jesus conquered death.

 Bible reference

JOHN 20:1–29

 Key verse

JOHN 20:16

Then Jesus said to her, 'Mary!'

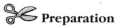 **Preparation**

Cards or OHP acetates with the following texts:

He is risen.
He is risen indeed.

At the appropriate moment, half the assembly (Chorus 1) should say, 'He is risen!' and the other half (Chorus 2) should respond with, 'He is risen indeed'. One method of doing this is to have two cards lifted up at the appropriate moment. The card holders will need a script to follow.

★★★

CAST

Two leaders / narrators (A and B)

STORY

A	On the day we now call Good Friday, Jesus' body was laid to rest. His tomb was rather like a small cave cut out of the rock. To make it secure, a large stone was rolled in front of the entrance.
B	On the day we now call Easter Day, Mary from Magdala got up very early—so early that it was still dark. She made her way to the garden. By the time she reached the cave, the sun was just rising. As she turned a corner in the garden, she saw the most amazing thing…
Chorus 1	He is risen!
Chorus 2	He is risen indeed!
A	The huge stone in front of the cave tomb had been rolled away. Mary was too frightened to look into the cave. She turned and ran back the way she had come.
B	Back in the city, trying hard to catch her breath, she spoke to Peter and John. 'They have taken the Lord from the tomb! We don't know where they have put him.'
A	It was Peter and John's turn to run! They ran side by side most of the way, but John was the fittest and he got to the cave first. He stood outside, looking into the cave.

B	John saw the strips of cloth, which had been wound round Jesus' body, lying inside.
Chorus 1	He is risen!
Chorus 2	He is risen indeed!
A	Peter came panting up and rushed, just like Peter always did, straight into the cave. John joined him. They were speechless. Jesus wasn't there! They hurried back to tell the others.
Chorus 1	He is risen!
Chorus 2	He is risen indeed!
B	Meanwhile, Mary had returned more slowly to the garden again. Peter and John had gone by the time she got there. Poor Mary really didn't know what to do. She wanted to say goodbye to Jesus but now his body had disappeared.
A	Through her tears, Mary looked into the cave. Inside were two angels dressed in white.
B	'Why are you crying?' asked the angels.
A	'They have taken Jesus' body away,' she said. 'I don't know where they have put him.'

Chorus 1	He is risen!
Chorus 2	He is risen indeed!
B	Perhaps she saw a shadow. Perhaps she heard a sound. Something made Mary turn round. Standing there was a man.
A	'Why are you crying?' asked the man. 'Who are you looking for?'
B	Mary thought he must be the gardener. She said, 'Sir, if you have taken his body away, please tell me, so I can go and get him.'
A	The man spoke just one word. 'Mary,' he said.
B	It was Jesus. Mary turned to face him. 'Teacher,' she said in amazement.
Chorus 1	He is risen!
Chorus 2	He is risen indeed!
A	'Now,' said Jesus, 'go and tell the others.'
B	Once again Mary returned to the city. This time her feet must have floated over the ground. She was so happy. Jesus was alive. She couldn't wait to tell the others.

 Reproduced with permission from *Year-round assemblies* published by BRF 2003 (1 84101 328 5)

Chorus 1	He is risen!
Chorus 2	He is risen indeed!
A	Later that day, all of Jesus' friends were together in a room. It may well have been the same upper room in which they had celebrated Passover.
B	While they were talking about what had happened, Jesus appeared and greeted them. They were very frightened.

A	'Why are you frightened?' asked Jesus. 'Look at my hands and feet and see who I am.'
B	His friends saw the scars on his hands and feet, from when he was nailed to the cross. Jesus' friends were so happy to see him alive again. Now they really did believe.
Chorus 1	He is risen!
Chorus 2	He is risen indeed!
A	But Thomas, one of his friends, was not with them. The others told him that they had seen Jesus. Thomas just couldn't believe them.

B	'Unless I see the scars for myself, I won't believe it!' he said.
A	A week later, the friends of Jesus were all together again. This time Thomas was with them. Once again Jesus appeared. He spoke to Thomas. 'Look at my hands,' he said. 'Stop doubting and have faith.'
B	And Thomas said, 'You are my Lord and my God!'
Chorus 1	He is risen!
Chorus 2	He is risen indeed!
A	Jesus said, 'Thomas, do you have faith in me because you have seen me? The people who have faith in me without seeing me are the ones who are really blessed.'
B	Christians have faith in Jesus. Although his death and resurrection happened two thousand years ago, Christians believe he is with them today.
A	On Easter Day, this greeting will be heard in Christian churches.
Chorus 1	He is risen!
Chorus 2	He is risen indeed!

★ ★ ★ ★ ★ **PRAYER** ★ ★ ★ ★ ★

Lord God, Easter is all about a new start. Sometimes we need a new start because things haven't gone as they should. Give us the strength to start again when we need to. Amen

EXTENSION MATERIAL

HYMNS

22   Lord of the dance
129   Jesus in the garden
130   All in an Easter garden
131   Now the green blade rises

PSHCE LINKS

Key Stage 1
2a, 4b, 4c, 4d

Key Stage 2
1a, 2a, 2e, 4a, 4b

SUGGESTED ACTIVITIES

 Discuss how Thomas must have felt when the other disciples told him they'd seen Jesus alive. What must he have thought?

 After the events of Easter, Thomas is often known as 'doubting Thomas'. Is this a fair name? Discuss as a group whether you think this is a fair reflection of what you know of the man.

 Draw the scene from the story where Mary discovers that Jesus' body is no longer there. What descriptions are given in the Bible readings? Use those to help you.

 Write an account of what Mary saw. Perhaps you might like to write an interview. What questions would you ask her?

 Act out a hot-seat situation, with someone playing the part of Mary and the rest of the class asking her questions about what happened to her.

 Act out the conversation between Mary and Peter and John when she tells them that Jesus' body has gone and that she's seen him alive. What would they say and how would they say it?

INTRODUCTION TO THE SUMMER TERM

This term's assemblies are built around Peter, beginning with his invitation to follow Jesus. Peter witnesses the healing of Jairus' daughter, is present at the transfiguration and then from the mountain-top descends to his denial at Jesus' trial. Peter is reassured by Jesus at the breakfast on the beach and speaks out on the day of Pentecost, with an amazing result. Peter's work for God continues with healing a lame man, understanding that the Christian faith is universal and getting into and out of prison.

The 'Fisherman, follower and friend' song provides a convenient summary each week of the content of the assemblies.

The final assembly of the term is an act of celebration, bringing together the work of the three terms.

FISHERMAN, FOLLOWER AND FRIEND

Peter was a fisherman,
A fisherman, a fisherman,
Peter was a fisherman,
Who sailed on Galilee.

Peter was a follower,
A follower, a follower,
Peter was a follower,
For Christ said, 'Follow me'.

Peter was a loving friend,
A loving friend, a loving friend,
Peter was a loving friend,
With John and James made three.

Peter said he didn't know,
Didn't know, didn't know,
Peter said he didn't know.
'But you're from Galilee!'

Peter ran fast to the tomb,
To the tomb, to the tomb,
Peter ran fast to the tomb,
To find it was empty.

Peter spoke at Pentecost,
Pentecost, Pentecost,
Peter spoke at Pentecost,
With the Spirit's certainty.

Peter saw the beggar man,
Beggar man, beggar man,
Peter saw the beggar man,
You can walk, trust me.

Peter locked up in the jail,
In the jail, in the jail,
Peter locked up in the jail.
The angel set him free.

Peter was a fisherman,
A follower, a friend.
Peter was a fisherman,
When Christ said 'Follow me'.

Fisherman, Follower and Friend

Music by Jo Dobbs
Lyrics by Brian Ogden

Pe - ter was a fish - er - man, a fish - er - man, a fish - er - man,

Pe - ter was a fish - er - man, who sailed on Ga - li - lee.

FOLLOW ME

 Theme

Jesus invites Simon Peter to be a disciple. There are many reasons why we choose our friends and are chosen as friends.

 Aim

To show how people started to follow Jesus first of all through John the Baptist. To examine the changes needed in order to follow Jesus full-time.

 Bible reference

JOHN 1:40–42

> **Key verse**
>
> JOHN 1:41
> *'We have found the Messiah!'*

 Preparation

A card or OHP acetate showing the following words is needed.

'Fisherman, follower and friend'

The words 'Fisherman, follower and friend' are the children's response whenever the leader says 'Simon' or 'Simon Peter'.

Copy the map on page 117 on to card or on to an OHP acetate. The map shows the main details of first-century Israel, including Lake Galilee, Capernaum, Bethlehem, Nazareth and Jerusalem.

★★★

CAST

Two leaders / narrators (A and B)

STORY

A   In our assemblies last term, we learnt about the life of Jesus. This term we shall learn about SIMON PETER—the fisherman who became a follower and friend of Jesus.

B   Hundreds of fishermen made their living by fishing in Lake Galilee. The lake, as we heard last term, was thirteen miles long and eight miles wide.

A   The people who lived near the lake ate fish rather than meat. Some of the fish was salted and sent to the larger towns.

B   The fishermen used two kinds of nets, one from a boat and one from the shore. The trawl net used on a boat was dragged through the water and then drawn together.

A The other net was much smaller. It was a hand-net, shaped rather like an umbrella. Weights were tied round the edge so that the net sank quickly over the fish. It took a lot of skill to use a hand-net.

B SIMON and Andrew were brothers. They were also skilled fishermen. They knew the lake, how to sail their boat, and how to use a hand-net. Fishing was what they were best at.

A Soon something was going to happen that would change their lives completely. It began not with SIMON, but with Andrew.

B Andrew took time off from fishing to go and listen to John the Baptist. John was teaching people about God and baptizing them in the River Jordan. Andrew was listening to John when Jesus walked by.

A John immediately stopped what he was doing. 'Here is the Son of God!' he said, pointing to Jesus.

B Andrew left John and followed Jesus. If Jesus was the Son of God, then Andrew wanted to know more about him.

A 'What do you want?' asked Jesus.

B 'Teacher,' asked Andrew, 'where do you live?' 'Come and see,' said Jesus. And Andrew spent the rest of the day with him.

A The next morning, Andrew couldn't wait to tell his brother, SIMON, what had happened. 'We have found the Messiah,' he said.

B Andrew didn't leave it at that. He took SIMON straight away to meet Jesus.

A When Jesus saw SIMON, he said a strange thing. 'SIMON, you will be called Peter.'

B All names have a meaning and Jesus gave SIMON a new name with a new meaning. The name Peter means 'a rock'.

A As well as a new name, Jesus gave SIMON a new job. From now on, he was going to catch people, not fish. SIMON PETER had spent years learning how to catch fish, so now he would have to spend time learning how to catch people.

B SIMON PETER would have been taught how to fish by his father. He and his brother

Andrew must have spent hours watching their father using the hand-net before he let them try it.

A They must have sailed the lake a thousand times before their father let them sail by themselves. They must have spent hours repairing the holes in the nets.

B They must have had many cold nights on the lake when they caught no fish. They learned patience and courage on Lake Galilee. Now someone had come along and invited them to use that patience and courage in a different sort of fishing.

A Jesus saw that SIMON PETER had what it would take to become a disciple. Peter didn't hesitate. He didn't say, 'I'll think about it and let you know.' SIMON PETER, together with Andrew, James and John, left everything and followed Jesus.

B They had a lot to learn, and during this term we shall see how SIMON PETER became a follower and friend of Jesus. Just as he had stormy and peaceful times as a fisherman on the lake, so SIMON PETER had his ups and downs as a disciple of Jesus.

 Reproduced with permission from *Year-round assemblies* published by BRF 2003 (1 84101 328 5)

A   Before meeting Jesus, the whole of SIMON PETER's life had taken place on and around Lake Galilee. Now his world was about to grow.

Show map.

B   This map shows some of the more important places visited by Jesus and his followers.

A   SIMON PETER lived in Capernaum at the northern end of Lake Galilee. It was to Capernaum that Jesus came from Nazareth to start his work.

B   Further south lies the town of Bethlehem. King David was born in Bethlehem. Joseph and Mary had to travel from Nazareth to Bethlehem, a distance of eighty miles, to be registered. It was where Jesus was born.

A   Five miles from Bethlehem is the city of Jerusalem. Jesus visited Jerusalem as a boy. He returned to Jerusalem as a man. It was outside Jerusalem that Jesus was crucified.

B   'Follow me,' said Jesus to SIMON PETER. His adventures were just beginning.

★ ★ ★ ★ ★ **PRAYER** ★ ★ ★ ★ ★

Dear God, thank you for friendships, for people we can trust and rely on. Help us to be trustworthy and reliable in return. Amen

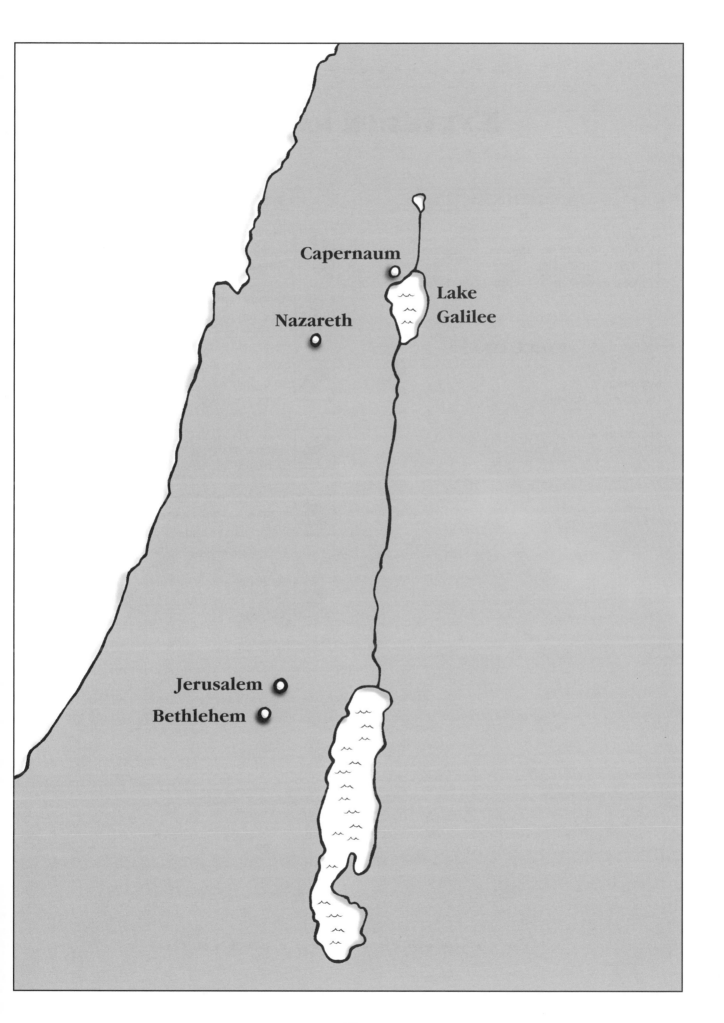

Capernaum

Lake
Galilee

Nazareth

Jerusalem

Bethlehem

 Reproduced with permission from *Year-round assemblies* published by BRF 2003 (1 84101 328 5)

EXTENSION MATERIAL

HYMNS

42 Travel on
43 Give me oil in my lamp
45 The journey of life
47 One more step

PSHCE LINKS

Key Stage 1
1b, 2a, 2b, 2c, 4a, 4b

Key Stage 2
1a, 2e, 4b, 4c, 4f

SUGGESTED ACTIVITIES

 Discuss the various responsibilities and skills required to be a fisherman in Jesus' time. How does this differ from what you thought?

 Discuss what you think made Andrew take time off from his fishing to go and hear John the Baptist.

 Write a list of the things that would have had to change in the lives of Andrew and Simon Peter when they started to follow Jesus.

 Write an imagined conversation between Andrew and Simon Peter, as Andrew tries to persuade him to go and hear Jesus.

 Research the average day of a modern fisherman. What expectations did you have beforehand, and how might these have changed in light of what you have found out?

 Research some meanings for names. What does your own name mean? Is it appropriate for you?

FEELINGS AND HEALINGS

Theme

Jesus heals people both by his actions and their faith. Jairus turned to Jesus for help. It is important to know who can help when help is needed.

Aim

To show that people can be helped in many different ways, including by faith in God.

Bible reference

LUKE 8:40–56

Key verse

LUKE 8:50

'Don't worry! Have faith, and your daughter will get well.'

Preparation

The story may be mimed by the rest of the class.

★★★

CAST

Three narrators
Jesus
Peter, James, John
Crowd
Jairus
Jairus' daughter
Messenger
Woman who is unwell
Wailing women

STORY

Narrator 1 As soon as Jesus had chosen his friends, he began his work. He…

Narrator 2 …taught people about the kingdom of God. He…

Narrator 3 …healed many people who were unwell or dying. He…

Narrator 1 …spent time with his friends, the disciples. One little story shows how much he cared for his friends.

Narrator 2 One Sabbath day, just after Jesus had been speaking in the synagogue in Capernaum, he went to Peter's home. Perhaps he was expected for lunch.

Narrator 3 When he arrived at the house, he was told that Simon Peter's mother-in-law was very ill. She had a high fever.

Narrator 1 Jesus went over to her and stood by her bed. He spoke to her. The fever left her and in no time she got up and cooked a meal.

Narrator 2 This must have been a very special moment for Peter. Peter soon became the leader among the disciples. He often spoke for the others if there was a question they wanted to ask Jesus. If Jesus

Reproduced with permission from *Year-round assemblies* published by BRF 2003 (1 84101 328 5)

wanted a small group of friends to go with him, he chose Peter, James and John.

Enter Jesus with Peter, James and John. Jesus mimes taking the three disciples to one side.

Narrator 3   Jesus soon became very popular with the ordinary people. Wherever he went, crowds followed him. They loved to hear his stories. They longed to see him heal those who were unwell. They never left Jesus alone.

Enter crowd. Jairus pushes his way through the crowd.

Narrator 1   One day, a man pushed his way through the crowd and knelt down in front of Jesus. The man's name was Jairus. Jairus was an important man. He was in charge of the synagogue—the place of worship.

Jairus kneels in front of Jesus.

Narrator 2   'My daughter is going to die,' Jairus said. 'Please come and place your hand on her. Then she will live.'

Narrator 3   Jairus was desperate. The girl was his only daughter. She was twelve years old. Jairus had heard how Jesus had made people well. Perhaps, just perhaps, Jesus could heal his daughter.

Narrator 1   Jesus turned to go with Jairus to his home. But then, to Jairus' dismay, Jesus stopped. He had felt a slight tug on his clothes.

Woman tugs Jesus' clothes.

Narrator 2   'Who touched me?' asked Jesus. It seemed a strange question. There were so many people crowding round to see Jesus.

Peter shows large crowd.

Narrator 3   'Master,' said Peter, 'people are pushing you from every side.' But Jesus knew that someone in the crowd needed him very badly.

Narrator 1   It was a woman who was very unwell who had touched his clothes. The moment she touched Jesus, she had been made better. Now she came in front of Jesus and knelt down.

Woman kneels.

Narrator 2   The crowd pushed even closer to see what would happen next. The woman stood and spoke.

Woman stands.

Narrator 3   'I have been ill for twelve years,' she told Jesus. 'I have spent a fortune on doctors. None of them

Reproduced with permission from *Year-round assemblies* published by BRF 2003 (1 84101 328 5)

has been able to help me. That's why I came to you. I just touched you and I was made well.'

Narrator 1 'You are now well because of your faith,' said Jesus. 'May God give you peace.'

Enter messenger from Jairus' house.

Narrator 2 Poor Jairus stood there watching all this happen. Someone came running up from his home. Then he got the news he dreaded most of all.

Narrator 3 'Your daughter has died! Why bother the teacher any more?' But Jesus too heard the message.

Narrator 1 'Don't worry,' he said. 'Have faith, and your daughter will get well.'

Mime Jesus, his disciples, Jairus and the messenger moving to house. Enter wailing women.

Narrator 2 At last they reached the house. Jesus asked Peter, James and John to go with him as he went in. Inside the house, everyone was quite sure the girl was dead.

Jesus beckons Peter, James and John to join him.

Narrator 3 It was the custom, when someone died, to have a group of women who wept and wailed. This wailing was like a low constant screaming.

Women wail.

Narrator 1 As Jesus entered the house, the wailing stopped. 'The child isn't dead,' said Jesus. 'She is just asleep.'

Narrator 2 The group of wailing women laughed. They knew the girl was

dead. Jesus told the women to leave the house.

Wailing women move out.

Narrator 3 Jesus took the girl's mother and father, together with his friends, into the room where the girl was lying. Jesus stood by the girl and took her hand.

Jesus moves to girl.

Narrator 1 'Little girl, get up,' he said. Immediately she sat up and started to walk around the room. 'Give her something to eat,' said Jesus.

Girl gets up and walks around.

★ ★ ★ ★ ★ **PRAYER** ★ ★ ★ ★ ★

Loving God, it's hard to understand illness and death. We pray for any of our friends or relations who are unwell at this time. Amen

Reproduced with permission from *Year-round assemblies* published by BRF 2003 (1 84101 328 5)

EXTENSION MATERIAL

HYMNS

22 Lord of the dance
23 Jesus, good above all other
24 Go, tell it on the mountain
26 Jesus Christ is here

PSHCE LINKS

Key Stage 1
1b, 1c, 2a, 2b, 4a, 4b, 4d

Key Stage 2
1a, 2a, 2e, 4a, 4b

SUGGESTED ACTIVITIES

 Discuss how Simon Peter must have felt when he knew his mother-in-law was very ill. Contrast this with how he must have felt after Jesus had healed her. What would he have felt about Jesus?

 Discuss the feelings and the faith of the woman who touched Jesus' clothes.

 Write down how Jairus felt when he heard the news that his daughter had died. How might he have felt towards the woman who held Jesus up?

 Act out a conversation between someone who witnessed Jesus healing the girl and a friend who wasn't there and doesn't believe what they're hearing.

 Research some modern examples of people who have been healed by faith. What conclusions can you draw about their stories?

ON THE MOUNTAIN-TOP

 Theme

Jesus is given reassurance that he is doing God's will. Everyone needs support and encouragement at one time or another.

 Aim

To understand how, as Jesus turned to go to Jerusalem, he was supported and encouraged not only by heroes of the past but by God, his father.

 Bible reference

LUKE 9:28–37

 Key verse

LUKE 9:35

'This is my chosen Son. Listen to what he says!'

 Preparation

No special preparation is needed for this assembly.

★★★★★★★★★★★★★★★★★★★★★★★★★★★★★★

CAST

Two leaders / narrators (A and B)

STORY

A Jesus didn't have many quiet moments to himself. If it wasn't the crowd demanding stories or miracles or healing, then it was his own friends asking him questions.

B Early one morning, Jesus went off by himself to pray. He knew that time was running out. All too soon he would have to go to Jerusalem to face death. But first he wanted to know if people were beginning to understand who he was and why he had come.

A When his disciples came to him, Jesus asked them a very important question. 'What do people say about me?'

B His disciples had spoken to many people in the crowds. They had heard the whispers that went round.

A 'Master, some say that you are John the Baptist come back to life again.' John had been murdered by King Herod a few months before.

B 'Some say that you must be Elijah.' Elijah was the greatest of all the prophets. God had often used prophets to speak to his people in the past.

A 'Others think that you might be one of the other prophets come back to life again.' Then Jesus looked them in the face and asked the most important question.

B 'But who do you say I am?' Jesus wanted to know if those who were closest to him had understood who he was. If none of them could answer the question, then all his work was for nothing. He waited for someone to answer. His friends looked at each other. Then…

A 'You are the Messiah sent from God!' said Peter. It was the answer Jesus was hoping for. One of his closest friends, the leader of the others, had understood who he was. His work had not failed, for Peter knew that Jesus was the Messiah, the Son of God.

B It was then that Jesus told his friends what would happen to him. 'The religious leaders will take me and kill me,' he said, 'but three days later I shall rise to life again.'

A His friends were devastated. They had spent months following Jesus. Now he was telling them that he would soon be put to death. Not only that, but if they remained true to him, then they might die too.

B A few days later, Jesus took Peter, James and John to a high mountain. We don't know for sure which mountain, but it was probably Mount Hermon. Mount Hermon rises to a height of over 9,000 feet.

A Night fell as they came to a stop high up the mountainside. Jesus knelt to pray. Peter, James and John pulled their coats around them and were soon asleep.

B Then an amazing thing happened. Jesus' clothes became a brilliant white. His face shone. Suddenly two figures appeared with Jesus.

A One was Moses. Moses was a great leader. He had led the Israelites out of Egypt. It was to Moses that God gave the Ten Commandments—the rules by which everyone should live.

B The second figure was Elijah. Elijah was the greatest of all the prophets. God had spoken to his people through Elijah. Moses and Elijah were two of the greatest heroes from the past. Now they were here on the mountain with Jesus.

A Moses and Elijah spoke with Jesus about his death in Jerusalem and all that it would mean. It was as though God had sent them to encourage Jesus.

B Peter and his two friends woke up to the sound of talking. They could hardly believe

A While Peter was speaking, a thick white cloud covered the mountain. Peter could see nothing. From out of the cloud there came a voice. Peter and his friends flung themselves to the ground.

B 'This is my own dear Son,' said the voice, 'and I am pleased with him. Listen to what he says.'

A As the voice died away, the cloud lifted. Moses and Elijah had gone. Only Jesus was standing there. 'Get up and don't be afraid,' he said to Peter and his friends.

B For a long time, Peter, James and John remained quietly thinking about what had happened. It had been a very special moment for Jesus and for them.

A But life had to go on, and the next day they came down from the mountain and were immediately met by a large crowd.

what they saw. Moses and Elijah were there on the mountain in front of them!

A Peter was confused, but as usual he felt he ought to do something. 'Master,' he blurted out, 'it is good for us to be here. Let us make three shelters, one for you, one for Moses and one for Elijah.'

B We all of us say things when we're frightened or confused. And Peter really didn't know what he was talking about.

★ ★ ★ ★ ★ PRAYER ★ ★ ★ ★ ★

God, the father of Jesus, thank you for your love. Give us strength to face whatever today will bring, so that at the end of the day we may have done our best. Amen

Reproduced with permission from *Year-round assemblies* published by BRF 2003 (1 84101 328 5)

EXTENSION MATERIAL

HYMNS

51 The Lord's Prayer
53 Peace, perfect peace
58 At the name of Jesus
140 The Peace prayer

PSHCE LINKS

Key Stage 1
1b, 1c, 2a, 4a, 4b, 4c

Key Stage 2
1a, 2e, 4a, 4b, 4c, 4f

SUGGESTED ACTIVITIES

 Discuss why we need to know what other people think and say about us. Does it make a difference to us?

 Discuss what it feels like when you are busy and want to have some time on your own.

 Draw the scene you imagine at the top of the mountain. You could link this to art history and look at how scenes from the Bible have been represented in the past.

 Write down some of the thoughts that Peter, James and John might have had after seeing Moses and Elijah on the top of the mountain.

 Act out how the disciples would have reacted to the news that Jesus was going to die soon. What would they have felt and said?

 Research some of the expressions that were used to describe Jesus. Look in both the Old and the New Testaments. Write them around a big drawing of Jesus.

I DON'T KNOW HIM!

 Theme
Peter's loyalty is tested to the limit. Loyalty to a good cause or to a friend needs to be understood and encouraged.

 Aim
To show how even Jesus' closest friends let him down at the crucial moment.

 Bible references
JESUS WASHES HIS DISCIPLES' FEET: JOHN 13:1–12
PETER'S DENIAL: MATTHEW 26:26–75

Key verse
MATTHEW 26:74
'I don't know that man!'

 Preparation
There are two possible mimes during this story. The first is the foot-washing, for which a towel is required. The second is Peter's denial.

★·★

CAST

Two leaders / narrators (A and B)
Twelve disciples (including Peter)
Jesus
Two girls who recognize Peter
Small crowd

STORY

A Jesus knew that the time had come to face the anger of the religious leaders in Jerusalem. He knew this would end in his death. As we heard last term, he shared a farewell meal with his friends in the upper room. Before the meal started, Jesus did a lovely thing.

B The roads in Palestine were not like ours. They were little more than mud. In dry weather they were deep in dust. In wet weather they were thick mud. Ordinary people wore sandals on their feet, which meant that after a journey their feet were either very dusty or very muddy.

Enter twelve disciples.

A   Because of that, there were water pots at the door of every house. As guests arrived, a servant washed the feet of the visitors and dried them with a towel.

Enter Jesus with towel.

B   Jesus' friends had been walking through the crowded streets of Jerusalem. Their feet would be far from clean. Jesus put a towel round his waist. He poured some water in a bowl. He went to each of his friends in turn and washed their feet.

Jesus kneels to wash Peter's feet.

A   Jesus knelt to wash Peter's feet. Peter couldn't believe what was happening. 'You will never wash my feet!' he said. Jesus said, 'If I don't wash you, you don't really belong to me.' Peter replied, 'Lord, don't wash just my feet. Wash my hands and my head.'

B   When Jesus had finished washing his friends' feet, he said, 'If your Lord and teacher has washed your feet, you should do the same for each other. I have set the example, and you should do for each other exactly what I have done for you.'

End of first mime. Second mime begins with Jesus and his disciples moving as if to the garden of Gethsemane.

A   During the meal, Jesus shared bread and wine with his friends. Christians have done this again and again for two thousand years. The service where this happens is called the Lord's Supper, the Eucharist, Holy Communion or the Mass. It takes place in Christian churches. It is the service during which Christians especially remember Jesus, his death on the cross, and his coming to life again.

B   After the meal, Jesus led his friends out of the city to the garden of Gethsemane. On the way he spoke to them. 'During this very night, all of you will reject me.'

A   Peter couldn't believe what Jesus had said. 'Even if all the others reject you, I never will!' he cried. Peter was quite sure he would never let Jesus down.

B   'I promise you,' said Jesus, 'that before a cock crows tonight, you will say three times that you don't know me.'

A   'Even if I have to die with you, I will never say I don't know you,' said Peter. And all the others said the same.

B   Jesus took Peter, James and John deeper into the garden. 'Stay here and keep awake with me,' he said. Jesus walked on a little way and knelt to pray to God his father. Peter and the others lay down. They couldn't keep awake and were soon fast asleep.

A   Jesus returned and woke them. 'Get up! Let's go,' he said. It was at that moment that the peace of the night was shattered. A large mob of people burst into the garden. Some were carrying clubs and some had swords.

 Reproduced with permission from *Year-round assemblies* published by BRF 2003 (1 84101 328 5)

B   Peter had taken a sword with him to the garden. He struck out at one of the men. Jesus said, 'Put your sword away.' Jesus knew that he had to do what God his father wanted.

A   At that moment, all of Jesus' friends ran off into the night. Despite their brave promises, not one was left—not even Peter. But Peter did follow at a distance. He saw that they took Jesus to the house of the high priest.

Jesus stands alone to one side of stage.

B   Outside the house was a courtyard. It was a cold night and someone had lit a fire. Peter crept nearer to the fire to warm himself. It was then that he was recognized.

Enter servant girl.

A   'You were with Jesus from Galilee,' said a servant girl.

B   'That isn't so! I don't know what you're talking about,' said Peter.

Enter second servant girl.

A   Peter moved away from the fire but he was seen by another servant girl. She told some of the people there, 'This man was with Jesus from Nazareth.'

B   'I don't even know the man!' said Peter hotly.

Enter small group.

A   A little while later, a small group of people walked over to Peter. 'We know that you are one of them. We can tell because you talk like someone from Galilee.'

Peter becomes very agitated.

B   Peter began to curse and swear. 'I don't know what you are talking about!' he shouted. As he was speaking he heard a cock crow.

Jesus looks at Peter—Peter is devastated.

A   At that very moment Jesus turned and looked at Peter. And Peter remembered that Jesus had said, 'Before a cock crows tomorrow morning, you will say three times that you don't know me.'

All exit.

B   Then Peter left the courtyard and wept bitterly.

★ ★ ★ ★ ★ **PRAYER** ★ ★ ★ ★ ★

Eternal God, forgive us when our courage lets us down and we fail ourselves or each other. Give us the strength to be loyal to who and what we believe in. Amen

EXTENSION MATERIAL

HYMNS

28 Judas and Mary
39 O Lord, all the world belongs to you
58 At the name of Jesus
62 Heavenly Father

PSHCE LINKS

Key Stage 1
1a, 1b, 1c, 1d, 2a, 2b, 4a, 4b

Key Stage 2
1a, 2a, 2e, 4a, 4b, 4c

SUGGESTED ACTIVITIES

 Discuss why Peter was the first to say that he wouldn't reject Jesus. What does this show you about the character of Peter?

 Discuss Peter's actions. Is it easy to say one thing and then to do another?

 Write an imaginary interview with Simon Peter after the cock crowed. What might you ask him and how would he reply?

 Act out a hot-seat situation with Peter in the hot seat. How does he react to what you ask him, and how does he feel after the denial?

 Discuss Jesus washing the feet of his disciples. He said that he was leading by example. Research any other people you know of who have led others by their example.

 Research the different forms of the service of breaking bread and sharing wine in the name of Jesus. These are known as the Lord's Supper, the Eucharist, Holy Communion or the Mass. How are they similar and how do they differ?

GONE FISHING

 Theme

Jesus appears to his friends by the lakeside and speaks with Peter. Peter acknowledges his disloyalty and the relationship is reestablished. Reestablishing relationships is never easy and usually needs forgiveness.

 Aim

To show how Jesus reassured Peter after his denial and, even after such failure, wanted Peter to continue following him.

 Bible reference

JOHN 21:1–19

> 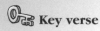 **Key verse**
>
> JOHN 21:7
>
> *'It's the Lord!'*

 Preparation

No special preparation is needed for this assembly.

★ ★

CAST

Four narrators
Seven fishermen (including Peter)
Jesus

STORY

Narrator 1 Last term we heard how Jesus was brought by the religious leaders to Pontius Pilate, the Roman Governor. He was taken to Golgotha and crucified on the day we call Good Friday. On Easter Day, Jesus came back to life again and was seen after that by many of his friends.

Narrator 2 'Don't leave Jerusalem yet,' Jesus told his friends. 'Wait here for the Father to give you the Holy Spirit, just as I told you he has promised to do.'

Narrator 3 Jesus' friends waited in Jerusalem as Jesus had directed them. They may even have stayed in the upper room where they had eaten their last meal with Jesus.

Narrator 4 After a time, Peter got restless. Peter was an action man. He wasn't good at just sitting around. One day he said to the others, 'I'm going fishing!'

The mime begins here with the seven fishermen.

Narrator 1 Thomas, Nathaniel, James, John and two more fishermen said, 'We're coming with you.' It was night as they pulled away from the shore. Night-time was usually the best time for fishing. But even with all their experience, they still caught nothing—not a single fish.

Mime fishing on the lake on the left-hand side of the imaginary boat.

Narrator 2 Then it happened. Just as the sun began to rise above the horizon, a figure appeared on the beach. He shouted the question every fisherman has been asked a thousand times. 'Have you caught anything?'

The figure of Jesus appears some distance away.

Narrator 3 They had to admit it. They had been out all night and not caught a thing. 'No,' they shouted back. But then the man on the shore said a strange thing.

Mime the negative reply.

Narrator 4 'Let your net down on the right side of the boat, and you will catch some fish.'

Mime change to right-hand side of the imaginary boat.

Narrator 1 They could have shouted back, 'What do you know about it?' They could have muttered to themselves, 'There's always someone who thinks he knows more about it than us.'

Narrator 2 But they didn't. This man seemed to know what he was talking about. They let their net down on the right side of the boat and could hardly believe what happened.

Mime struggle with net and disbelief of fishermen.

Narrator 3 The net was so full of fish that they couldn't drag it into the boat. It was then that John looked up. Perhaps the sun was higher, perhaps he could now see the man's face. Whatever had happened, John now knew for certain who it was.

Mime John's recognition of Jesus.

Narrator 4 'It's the Lord!' he shouted. When Peter heard this, he jumped straight into the water. He half swam and half waded the hundred metres to the shore. He just couldn't wait to see Jesus again.

Mime Peter jumping in to the sea.

Narrator 1 The other six friends stayed in the boat and, after a struggle, managed to drag the net ashore. As they landed, they saw that Jesus had made a fire. 'Bring some of the fish,' said Jesus.

Mime dragging net.

Narrator 2 Peter helped the others with the net. Soon there was the delicious smell of fish cooking over the fire. Jesus had brought bread and he gave some of it to his friends. They ate it with the fish.

Mime cooking over the fire and eating.

Narrator 3 After breakfast, Jesus and Peter went for a walk along the shore. There were questions Jesus wanted to ask Peter.

Mime Jesus and Peter in conversation.

Narrator 4 'Peter, do you love me?'

Narrator 1 'Yes, Lord, you know I do,' said Peter.

Narrator 2 They walked a little further.

Narrator 4 'Peter, do you love me?' asked Jesus a second time.

Narrator 1 'Yes, Lord, you know I love you,' said Peter.

Narrator 3 They walked a little further still. Again Jesus looked at Peter.

Narrator 4 'Peter, do you love me?' asked Jesus a third time.

Narrator 1 Peter was hurt that Jesus had asked him the same question three times. 'Lord, you know everything. You know I love you.'

Narrator 2 Jesus looked at Peter again. He said words that must have taken Peter back to the time, three years before, when he first met Jesus. 'Follow me.'

End of mime.

Narrator 3 Perhaps it was then, or perhaps it was later on, that Peter remembered something else. When Jesus was taken before the high priest, Peter had sworn that he didn't know Jesus. Three times he had said it. Now Jesus had asked him three times if Peter loved him. Now he knew that Jesus had forgiven him.

Narrator 4 The breakfast on the beach was a very special time for Peter.

Narrator 1 Soon after this, Jesus met with some of his friends on a hill in Galilee. It was by Lake Galilee that he had first met most of them. It was in Galilee that he said farewell to them.

Narrator 2 Jesus told them again to wait for the coming of the Holy Spirit. After giving them his blessing, he was hidden by a cloud and taken to heaven. His friends returned to Jerusalem to wait for the Holy Spirit to come.

★ ★ ★ ★ ★ **PRAYER** ★ ★ ★ ★ ★

Jesus, thank you that your loyalty never failed. Sometimes we are disloyal to friends or family or to what we really believe in. Help us to understand what we have done and try harder next time. Amen

EXTENSION MATERIAL

HYMNS

87   Give us hope, Lord
92   When night arrives
99   Love will never come to an end
106 It's a new day

PSHCE LINKS

Key Stage 1
1c, 2a, 4a, 4b, 4c, 4d

Key Stage 2
1a, 2e, 4a, 4b, 4c

SUGGESTED ACTIVITIES

 Discuss the sort of things that the friends of Jesus might have said and thought as they waited in Jerusalem. What different emotions would they have experienced?

 Discuss what it is like to be hurt by someone, and to be able to forgive them. What does forgiveness entail? Is it easy? Why? Does it depend on how much you've been hurt?

 Three times Jesus asked Peter if he loved him. Discuss the various types of love that there are within human relationships.

 Write a play based on the assembly. Who will be in it, and what will they say, do and think? How will you make the characters convincing?

 Draw or paint a picture of the moment the net comes up full of fish. What will the faces of Jesus' friends look like? What expressions do you expect they would have had?

 Write a prayer asking for forgiveness. Say how you feel and what you are asking forgiveness for.

 Act out the conversation that might have taken place as John identifies Jesus. What might the other friends have said?

WIND AND FIRE

 Theme

A day of huge changes. The disciples were changed, the church was formed and nothing would ever be the same again. Change is possible in all situations.

 Aim

To show that the promises Jesus made did come true and that his followers became changed men. Fear had gone, courage had come, enough to change the world.

 Bible references

JESUS IS TAKEN TO HEAVEN: ACTS 1:1–13

THE COMING OF THE HOLY SPIRIT: ACTS 2:1–47

 Key verse

ACTS 2:4

The Holy Spirit took control of everyone.

 **Preparation**

Two cards or OHP acetates are needed, each with one of the following questions:

'What does it mean?'
'What should we do?'

The two questions are used as an interactive response by the children during the story.

★★★

CAST

Two leaders / narrators (A and B)

STORY

A   Fifty days after the feast of Passover, there is another great religious festival. It is called Pentecost. Pentecost means 'fiftieth'. It is the main harvest festival.

B   Just as for Passover, the city of Jerusalem was crowded with people who had come for the festival. Just like our harvest festival, it was a time of great thanksgiving for God's gifts at harvest.

A   The festival took place at the beginning of June. It was the best time in the year to travel and people had come from many different countries to celebrate the festival in Jerusalem. The day itself was a holiday and the streets were packed.

B Jesus' friends were gathered together in a building in the city. It might have been the upper room. They were all there, all Jesus' friends, in that one place. Peter, James and John, the other disciples and many of the women who knew Jesus all crowded together.

A They were waiting for what Jesus had promised before he had been taken to heaven—the Holy Spirit. They didn't know what it would be like but they knew that it would be a very special moment.

B It started with the noise of a wind. The noise got louder and louder and seemed to swirl around them, even though they were inside the house.

A The wind was followed by tongues of fire. The fire didn't burn but it did settle for a moment on each one of them. The Holy Spirit took control of everyone. They all spoke in different languages.

B The noise of the great wind had been heard outside the house. In a moment a huge crowd had gathered to see what had happened. The crowd began to get excited…

All 'What does it mean?'

B …they asked. 'Why are they all speaking in different languages?'

A 'It's just a joke,' said some of them. 'They've had too much to drink. They're drunk, that's what it is!' Peter stood up and the crowd went silent…

All 'What does it mean?'

B 'Listen carefully to what I say,' said Peter. You are wrong if you think we are drunk. After all, it's only nine o'clock in the morning. Remember what Joel the prophet said. "When the last days come I will give my Spirit to my servants, both men and women."'

All 'What does it mean?'

A The crowd knew the words that Peter quoted from the book of Joel. But Peter hadn't finished. He wanted to bring them up to date and tell them about Jesus.

B 'God proved that he sent Jesus to you by having him perform miracles, wonders and signs. All of you know this. Evil men put Jesus to death on a cross. But God set him free from death and raised him to life. Death could not hold him in its power.'

All 'What does it mean?'

A The crowd were listening intently. What Peter was saying made sense to them. Peter finished what he was saying with these words: 'Everyone in Israel should know then for certain that God has made Jesus both Lord and Christ, even though you put him to death.'

B When the people heard what Peter said, they were very upset. They asked Peter…

All 'What should we do?'

A 'Turn back to God!' answered Peter. 'Understand that you have done wrong things—and be sorry for them. Be baptized in the name of Jesus Christ, so that your sins will be forgiven. Then you will be given the Holy Spirit. It is for everyone that our Lord God will choose, no matter where they live.'

 Reproduced with permission from *Year-round assemblies* published by BRF 2003 (1 84101 328 5)

B Peter told them many other things as well. He had learnt a great deal during the three years he had spent with Jesus. Now he could pass those things on to others. Now at last was the opportunity to do what Jesus had called him to do. Now at last, he really was fishing for people.

All 'What should we do?'

A On that day about three thousand people believed what Peter had said and were baptized. They spent their time learning from the friends of Jesus, they prayed together and shared bread and wine, just as Jesus had done.

B It was a wonderful time. People sold what they had and gave money to whoever needed it. They shared their food. Every day, more people became followers of Jesus. The coming of the Holy Spirit at Pentecost had made all the difference to the little group of Jesus' friends.

✫ ✫ ✫ ✫ ✫ **PRAYER** ✫ ✫ ✫ ✫ ✫

Spirit of God, thank you for Pentecost. Sometimes we need to make big changes. Please give us the courage to do so. Amen

---

EXTENSION MATERIAL

HYMNS

24   Go, tell it on the mountain
27   A man for all the people
100   I may speak
107   You've got to move

PSHCE LINKS

Key Stage 1
1b, 2a, 4a, 4b, 4c

Key Stage 2
1a, 2a, 2e, 4a, 4b

SUGGESTED ACTIVITIES

 Discuss with some friends how the disciples must have felt at that time. What emotions would they have experienced?

 Discuss modern-day evangelism. What evidence is there to show that people are converted to Christianity? Look at the lives of some of the more well-known evangelists.

 Write a newspaper report about what happened that morning. How will you present the information? Will you 'interview' the disciples, or passers-by? How will you convince your 'readers' that it actually happened?

 Draw a cartoon strip of what happened in the story. How will you tell your own version?

 Write a diary account as if you were a member of the crowd. What did you hear and what did you see? How can you make it realistic?

 Devise and act out a drama of the events of that morning. How will you make it realistic? What things would be said?

 Research the feasts of Passover and Pentecost. What can you find out about them and how they would have been celebrated in the time of Jesus?

JUMPING FOR JOY

 Theme

Peter was asked for money but gave something far more valuable. Today's values sometimes need challenging.

 Aim

Peter heals the lame man and shows that Jesus' friends have great power through faith in him.

 Bible reference

ACTS 3:1–10

 Key verse

ACTS 3:6

'I will give you what I do have. In the name of Jesus Christ from Nazareth, get up and start walking.'

 Preparation

The story is told in the form of an interview with the lame man.

★★★★★★★★★★★★★★★★★★★★★★★★★★★★★★★★★★★★★★

 CAST

Narrator
Lame man

STORY

Narrator   As we heard last time, Peter spoke to huge crowds during the festival of Pentecost. The result was that many people became Christians and continued to learn about their new faith. One day, Peter and John were going into the great temple in Jerusalem. Sitting by the entrance was a man who was lame. Because of his lameness, all his life he had had to be a beggar. Let's imagine that he is with us today…

Enter lame man.

Narrator   Perhaps you could start by telling us a little about yourself.

Lame man	Well, you see, I have never been able to use my legs. I was born lame—I could never walk or run about like the other children. As I got older, I couldn't get any work.
Narrator	That's terrible. So what happened?
Lame man	There was nothing for it but to beg. For nearly thirty years I've sat by the door of the temple. You know the one—it's called the Beautiful Gate. Some friends carry me there each morning and take me home at night.
Narrator	But that day, something happened to change your life. Tell us, please, about Peter. Did he speak to you?
Lame man	No, it was me. I called out to him—as I call out to everyone who goes into the temple. I begged him to give me some money. Then he said something very strange. He said, 'Look up at me.'
Narrator	Did he give you some money? Was he generous?
Lame man	No he didn't, and yes he was. That's to say, he didn't give me any money, but he did give me something I've longed for all my life. He made me walk.
Narrator	That's amazing. You mean Peter cured you?
Lame man	Peter pulled me to my feet and I started walking and jumping about. Walking may not mean much to you but if you've sat and watched while others do the moving, believe me, it's a fantastic feeling.
Narrator	So did you run home and tell your friends all about it? I'm sure I would.
Lame man	No, I followed Peter into the temple. I was so happy. I was walking and jumping and praising God because he had healed me.

Narrator	It must have caused a bit of a scene in the temple. People would have recognized you.
Lame man	They certainly did. They knew I was the one who had been lying by the Beautiful Gate for all those years. They were amazed and joined me in praising God. Soon there was a huge crowd.
Narrator	Knowing Peter like we do, I expect he made the most of the moment to tell people about Jesus.
Lame man	All the people went quiet when he started to speak. He told them how Jesus had been put to death. He explained that Jesus had come back to life again. Then I saw, out of the corner of my eye, that there was going to be trouble. The temple guard had arrived. They looked furious.
Narrator	So it was beginning to look really bad. You don't play games with the temple guard—even I know that. Whatever happened?
Lame man	The temple guard, together with some of the priests, arrested Peter. They put him in jail for the night.

 Reproduced with permission from *Year-round assemblies* published by BRF 2003 (1 84101 328 5)

Then, for the first time ever, I walked home. The friends who normally carried me couldn't believe it. The next morning, I found where they had taken Peter.

Narrator That was very brave of you.

Lame man Peter had helped me and I wanted to help him. Peter was standing there surrounded by all the religious leaders. They were asking him lots of questions. Then he spoke and told them about Jesus. He said I had been healed because of the power that Jesus had given him.

Narrator How did all the officials take this? I should think it made them even angrier.

Lame man I could see how amazed they were. Here was a fisherman from Galilee standing up and speaking to the highest religious leaders in the land. They couldn't say I hadn't been healed. I was standing there with Peter—and I mean standing, not lying down as I used to do.

Narrator Yes, the proof was there—standing, as you say, in front of them. Peter, through the power of Jesus Christ, had healed you. So what happened next?

Lame man They sent us out of the room while they discussed what to do. They had a problem, as everyone in Jerusalem knew I had been healed. They couldn't say it never happened. So they took the bully's way out.

Narrator What do you mean, the bully's way?

Lame man They called us back in and told Peter he must never speak to anyone about the name of Jesus. Well, you've been learning about Peter, so you can imagine what he said. 'Do you think God wants us to obey you or him? We cannot keep quiet about what we have seen and heard.' There was nothing more to be said and Peter was set free.

Narrator They were certainly brave men and women, the first followers of Jesus. Thank you so much for telling us about your meeting with Peter at the Beautiful Gate.

★ ★ ★ ★ ★ **PRAYER** ★ ★ ★ ★ ★

Creator God, there are so many things in this world that we take for granted—good health, food, homes and school. Yet there are many people who have few of these things. Help us to be grateful for what we have and to care about those who have little. Amen

EXTENSION MATERIAL

HYMNS

30 Join with us
33 Praise the Lord in everything
37 O praise ye the Lord
40 Praise Him

PSHCE LINKS

Key Stage 1
1b, 2a, 2b, 2c, 4a, 4b, 4c

Key Stage 2
1a, 1c, 2a, 2e, 4a, 4b, 4c, 4f

SUGGESTED ACTIVITIES

 Discuss the beggar's actions when he heard that Peter was imprisoned. What did he do? What other examples can you think of when people have helped each other?

 Discuss what Peter might have done when the officials told him he was not to speak about Jesus. What were his reasons for disobeying them? Why might he have decided to keep quiet?

 Write a list of all the different times in a normal day when you can say 'thank you', and who you would be thanking. How often do you actually do it? Does making the list change the way you think?

 Write a prayer thanking God for some of the things in your life. What are you most grateful for? Is it something that people might consider ordinary?

 Act out what it is like not to be able to walk. Try doing 'ordinary' things. Can you manage it? What does it feel like? Was there anything that surprised you about your 'disability'?

 Research the story of the ten lepers (Luke 17:11–19). Compare the reactions of the nine who didn't thank God to the story of the beggar. What conclusions can you draw from each story?

IT'S FOR EVERYONE

 Theme

A turning point in Christian thinking—belief in Jesus was for everybody, not just those of the Jewish faith. Tolerance and understanding between those who speak different languages, are of a different race and follow different traditions is vital in today's world.

 Aim

To demonstrate how Peter was shown, both in a dream and through a visit, that the Christian faith was for all people.

 Bible reference

ACTS 10:1–48

 Key verse

ACTS 10:34

'Now I am certain that God treats all people alike.'

 Preparation

A sheet with outlines of pigs, cows, snakes and birds pinned to it. Templates for the animals are on page 149.

****

CAST

Four narrators
Peter
Tabitha
Cornelius and friends
Two men
Marching soldiers

STORY

Narrator 1   After what happened in Jerusalem, Peter left the city and travelled from place to place to speak to those who had become followers of Jesus.

Narrator 2   In the town of Joppa lived a lady called Tabitha. She was always doing kind things for those who were unwell or living in poverty. One day, Tabitha became ill and died.

Narrator 3   Now it happened that Peter was in the town of Lydda, which was only a short distance from Joppa.

Tabitha's friends heard that Peter was in Joppa and they sent two men to fetch him.

Mime begins here. Enter the two men who fetch Peter.

Narrator 4   'Please come as quickly as you can,' the men said to Peter. Immediately Peter went to Joppa. There he was taken to an upstairs room where Tabitha's body lay.

Peter kneels down by Tabitha.

Narrator 1   Peter sent everyone out of the room and knelt down to pray. He stood and spoke to Tabitha. 'Get up,' he told her.

Tabitha wakes up. Peter helps her to her feet.

Narrator 2   Tabitha opened her eyes and saw Peter standing there. She sat up and Peter helped her to her feet. Peter did not go back to Lydda but stayed on in Joppa.

Tabitha and Peter exit.

Narrator 3   Meanwhile, about 35 miles away, up the coast, something rather unusual was happening in Caesarea.

Narrator 4   Stationed in Caesarea was a part of the Italian regiment of the Roman army. The centurion's name was Cornelius. A centurion was in charge of one hundred men.

Enter some marching soldiers. Cornelius is in charge of them.

Narrator 1   Cornelius was a very religious man. He worshipped God, gave a lot of money to the poor and spent much time praying. One afternoon at about three o'clock…

Cornelius on his own, praying.

Narrator 2   …Cornelius had a vision or dream. He saw…

Enter angel.

Narrator 3   …an angel from God calling out…
Narrator 4   'Cornelius!'
Narrator 1   Cornelius was very surprised and stared at the angel. At last he found his voice and said, 'What is all this about?'

Narrator 2   'God has heard your prayers and knows about your gifts to the poor,' said the angel. 'God wants you to send men to Joppa to find a man called Peter.'

Angel exits. Cornelius calls two men.

Narrator 3   The angel left, and Cornelius called in two of his most trusted men. He explained to them what had happened and sent them off to Joppa.

Cornelius and men exit.

Narrator 4   Meanwhile, back in Joppa, Peter went on to the roof of the house where he was staying. It was quiet up there and he had a good view of the sea. It was midday and he could smell the lunch cooking below him.

Enter Peter, who falls asleep.

Narrator 1   It was so quiet that he fell asleep. Just as Cornelius had done, Peter too had a dream. In his dream he saw a huge sheet, held up by its four corners. Peter looked into the sheet.

A sheet is brought on, with pictures of various animals pinned to it.

Narrator 2   In the sheet were all kinds of animals, snakes and birds. A voice spoke to Peter, 'Peter, get up. Kill these and eat them.'

Narrator 3   But Peter said, 'Lord, I can't do that. I've never eaten anything that is unclean and not fit to eat.'

Narrator 4   The voice spoke again. 'When God says that something can be used for food, don't say it isn't fit to eat.'

Narrator 1   This happened three times before the sheet was taken away. Peter woke and was still wondering what his dream meant when there was a knock on the door.

Peter wakes. There is the sound of a knock on the door. Enter men from Cornelius.

Narrator 2   It was the men sent by Cornelius. Peter went downstairs and spoke to the men. 'Why have you come?' he asked.

Peter and men in conversation.

Narrator 3   'Centurion Cornelius sent us,' they said. 'He is a good man who worships God and is liked by the Jewish people. One of God's angels told him to send for you.'

Narrator 4   The next day, they all set out for Caesarea, where Cornelius was waiting for them…

Cornelius and group of friends and relatives enter.

Narrator 4   …Cornelius greeted Peter and took him inside his house. There Peter met Cornelius' friends and relatives.

Peter and men meet Cornelius.

Narrator 1   First Peter spoke. 'You know that we Jews are not allowed to have anything to do with people who

Show sheet with animals again.

Narrator 1 The meaning of the parable—the dream—was that the good news about Jesus should be shared with everyone. And here, as if to prove it, was a Roman centurion who believed in God and wanted to learn about Jesus.

Narrator 2 Peter told them about Jesus, his teaching, his death and his coming back to life again. When he finished speaking, Cornelius and his friends were baptized.

Peter leads Cornelius and everyone else off stage.

Narrator 3 It was a very important moment in the story of how people all over the world came to hear about Jesus.

Narrator 4 Peter stayed with them in Caesarea for a few days and then went to Jerusalem to tell the other Christian leaders what had happened.

are not Jews. But God has shown me that is wrong. Now, please tell me why you sent for me.'

Narrator 2 Cornelius told Peter about his dream—how the angel had told him to send to Joppa for Peter. 'We are here to learn what God has to say through you,' he said.

Narrator 3 Up until then, the friends of Jesus believed that Jesus had only come to Jewish people. They had no idea that the good news that Jesus brought was for everybody in the whole world.

Narrator 4 That was why Peter's dream was so important. It was a sort of parable—a story to teach something new. The Jews believed that only certain animals were fit to eat. God told Peter in the dream that he could eat any animal.

★ ★ ★ ★ ★ **PRAYER** ★ ★ ★ ★ ★

Father of all, you have made people to be of many colours, languages and traditions. Help us to live together as one family—to respect and to care for one another. Amen

Reproduced with permission from *Year-round assemblies* published by BRF 2003 (1 84101 328 5)

Reproduced with permission from *Year-round assemblies* published by BRF 2003 (1 84101 328 5)

EXTENSION MATERIAL

HYMNS

66   In Christ there is no east or west
67   Black and white
69   Family of man
71   If I had a hammer

PSHCE LINKS

Key Stage 1
1a, 2a, 2c, 2f, 4a, 4b, 4c

Key Stage 2
1a, 2a, 2c, 2e, 4a, 4b, 4d, 4f

SUGGESTED ACTIVITIES

 Explore what it means when the narrator said, 'Cornelius was a very religious man'. What might you do if you were very religious, and how might you show it in your everyday life?

 Discuss what was unusual about Cornelius believing in God. What did most of the Roman soldiers believe in?

 A centurion was in charge of one hundred men. What other words can you find that begin with 'cent-' (which means 'one hundred')?

 Explore what the Jewish laws forbade them to eat. Draw up a chart of what Peter ate before the dream and what he ate afterwards.

 Research Christianity in different countries. Which aspects are the same as in this country, and which differ? Do they differ in the aspects that are fundamental to Christianity—for example, the teachings of Jesus?

 Using a map and some resource material, explore which countries in the world have Christian communities. Shade in these countries. Do the results surprise you? How?

 Research countries where Christianity is forbidden. What happens to Christians in these countries? Is this fair? Discuss how various organizations are trying to make changes in these situations.

IN AND OUT

 Theme

Peter was in a desperate situation, but he was rescued and continued his work. Some situations look so bad that there seems to be no solution, but giving up is never the answer.

 Aim

To show how Peter's amazing escape from prison showed clearly that God still had work for him to do.

 Bible reference

ACTS 12:1–19

 Key verse

ACTS 12:11

'I am certain that the Lord sent his angel to rescue me.'

 Preparation

The assembly takes the form of an interview with Peter.

★ ★

CAST

Narrator
Peter

STORY

Narrator   All this term, we have been hearing about the adventures of Peter from the time he gave up fishing to become a follower and friend of Jesus. Let's imagine that Peter himself is here with us today.

Peter   It is a great pleasure to be here. Although it is now many years ago, I can still remember those words that Jesus said to me. 'Follow me and you will bring in people instead of fish.'

Narrator   If you don't mind, we would really like you to tell us what happened after the meeting you had with the other Christian leaders in Jerusalem. I believe it was becoming very dangerous to be a follower of Jesus.

Peter   It was indeed. Many of my friends were killed. John's brother James was arrested by King Herod. Herod's soldiers took James and killed him. It was a very sad day and a great loss. Herod saw that this pleased the religious leaders and then had me arrested.

Narrator   That must have been terrifying. Please tell us what happened.

Peter   Herod wanted to be sure I didn't escape. He put me in jail and ordered not one but four squads of soldiers to guard me! I had a soldier on each side of me and two more were keeping watch on the entrance to the jail. They never left me, day or night.

Narrator   You must have thought that Herod would kill you just as he had killed James.

Peter   I had great faith that my friends would be praying for me. I know that God answers prayers and he certainly did this time. It all happened in the middle of the night. I was tied up by two great chains.

Narrator   So there was no way of escape. There was nothing you could do to get free.

Peter   I was sleeping when suddenly there was a very bright light in my prison cell. From out of the light stepped an angel. He poked me in the side and woke me up. 'Quick, get up!' he said. As he said it, my chains fell to the floor.

Narrator   Amazing! So God sent an angel to help you.

Peter   The angel told me to get dressed. I put on my sandals and then my coat. 'Follow me,' ordered the angel. I couldn't believe this was happening—I really thought it must be a dream.

Narrator   But what about the soldiers? Surely they tried to stop you?

Peter   No, not one of them moved. We walked past two groups of soldiers and came to the iron gate that led into the city. As we approached the gate, it opened by itself. I was out of prison and on the street. As we walked along, the angel disappeared as suddenly as he had arrived.

Narrator   So the angel did the work that God sent him to do, and you were free. But it couldn't have been very safe on the streets. You were well known—anyone could have reported you.

Peter   It was when the angel left that I finally realized what had happened. I knew that the Lord had sent his angel to rescue me

	from Herod and from everything the religious leaders were planning to do to me.
Narrator	Your friends must have been very worried about you. But where did you go from the prison?
Peter	The nearest safe house belonged to the mother of my friend John Mark. I was sure they would look after me. I walked up to the house and knocked on the gate. I heard someone come, but then it went silent again.
Narrator	So with the dawn breaking over the city, you were left on the street. So near but yet so far!
Peter	It was the maid, Rhoda. She had seen me but was too excited to open the gate. She rushed back to the others and told them that I was standing there. Well, they couldn't believe it. They said to Rhoda, 'You must be mad.'
Narrator	How frustrating for you. Safety was through the gate but no one would open it!
Peter	I kept on knocking and at last someone opened the gate. They were shouting and praising God.

	They were so delighted and happy to see me. I asked for quiet and told them how the Lord had led me out of jail.
Narrator	But you couldn't stay there, surely? Someone could so easily have seen you.
Peter	No, having told them the good news that I had escaped, I left and went to somewhere safe. I heard later that the soldiers came searching for me. I don't think Herod was very pleased with the soldiers who had been on guard in the jail, though.
Narrator	Peter, thank you so much for telling us about your adventures, both in and out of prison. Your story is very exciting.

★ ★ ★ ★ ★ **PRAYER** ★ ★ ★ ★ ★

Thank you, God, that Jesus never gave up on the work you sent him to do. Help us, even in really bad times, to keep going one step at a time. Amen

Reproduced with permission from *Year-round assemblies* published by BRF 2003 (1 84101 328 5)

EXTENSION MATERIAL

HYMNS

57 Lost and found
60 I listen and I listen
63 Spirit of God
65 When I needed a neighbour

PSHCE LINKS

Key Stage 1
1b, 2a, 2b, 2c, 4a, 4b, 4c

Key Stage 2
1a, 2a, 2e, 4a, 4b, 4c

SUGGESTED ACTIVITIES

 Discuss to what extent Herod was in a difficult position. He was being pressurized by the religious leaders to arrest and kill the followers of Jesus. Do you think he acted fairly?

 Discuss the qualities of friendship. What attributes did John Mark's mother show?

 Draw a picture of Peter's face. Around it, write all the differing things he must have thought during this story. What emotions would he have experienced?

 Write an interview with Rhoda. What will you ask her and how might she reply?

 Act out a hot-seat situation with Rhoda in the chair. What might she have said and what will you want to find out from her?

 Act out an interview with Herod. How would he have reacted to the news that, despite four guards around his cell and two strong chains, Peter had escaped?

 Research other times in the Bible when an angel was used either as a messenger or as a rescuer. How many different times can you think of?

CELEBRATION

 Theme

A reminder of the year's assemblies.

 Aim

To celebrate the lives of David, Peter and Jesus.

 Bible reference

There is no specific Bible reference for this assembly. You may wish to insert some of the key verses used throughout the assemblies into the narration as appropriate.

 **Preparation**

Response cards for the following interactive responses are needed:

David: 'Our hero'
Jesus: 'He is risen! He is risen indeed!'
Peter: 'Fisherman, follower and friend'

A time-line showing David, Jesus and Peter is also needed. The time-line on page 158 may be used.

The children will be required to produce large illustrations of some of the following for an exhibition for the final assembly:

- David
- King Saul
- Goliath
- Bathsheba
- Jesus the carpenter
- John the Baptist
- A Roman soldier
- Peter
- Fire and wind
- The lame man jumping for joy
- A prison cell
- Any other scenes from the stories of your choosing

★★★

CAST

Two narrators / leaders (A and B)

ASSEMBLY

A During the past year, we have looked at the lives of three people. In the autumn term it was David.

B In the spring term it was Jesus.

A And in the summer term it has been Peter.

B Today we are going to celebrate the lives of those three people by reminding ourselves of what they achieved.

A DAVID started life as a shepherd boy. He learned the skills he needed to keep his flock safe.

B DAVID was anointed by Samuel to be king in place of Saul. But it was to be a long and exciting time before that happened.

A DAVID defeated the giant Goliath and became very popular with the people. Because of his musical skills, he managed to calm King Saul's angry moods.

B But Saul became jealous and tried to kill DAVID on many occasions. DAVID and Saul's son Jonathan became friends, but the time came when DAVID had to run away to save his life.

A Both King Saul and Jonathan were killed in battle, and DAVID became king. He captured Jerusalem and built his palace there.

B DAVID behaved very badly with Bathsheba when he had her husband killed. But we remember DAVID for his courage, for his poetry and as a great king.

A In the Bible, Jesus is very often called Jesus, son of DAVID. We thought about this in the two weeks leading up to Christmas.

Sing: 'Good news, bad news'

B In the spring term, our assemblies were about the life of JESUS. He spent the first thirty or so years at home learning the skills of a carpenter.

A Meanwhile, his cousin, John the Baptist, was preparing the way for JESUS. Out in the desert he invited people to turn away from the things they did wrong and be baptized.

B JESUS was himself baptized by John, and then went through a testing time in the wilderness. Finally, JESUS started his work by gathering some friends around him.

A JESUS took his new friends to a wedding in Cana, where he saved the young couple from the embarrassment of running out of wine.

B JESUS often taught through stories called parables—the farmer and the seeds, the lost sheep, the good Samaritan, the house built on the rock, and many more.

A JESUS healed those who were unwell, and taught people about God in the synagogues and by the lakeside. But all the time, opposition from the religious leaders was growing.

B After about three years, JESUS deliberately turned towards Jerusalem, knowing that by doing so he was facing death. Before he left his friends, JESUS had a final meal with them.

A Today we call that meal the Lord's Supper, the Eucharist, Holy Communion or the Mass. Christians have never stopped remembering JESUS through this service.

B JESUS was deserted by his friends, tried, sentenced to death and marched through the streets of Jerusalem to be crucified.

A On the third day, the day we call Easter Sunday, JESUS returned to life and was seen by many of his friends.

All He is risen! He is risen indeed!

Sing: 'The busy day song'

B This term we have been following the life of PETER—the fisherman who became a friend of Jesus and the leader among Jesus' friends.

A Jesus invited PETER to change from catching fish to catching people. PETER had much to learn during those three years. He was, for example, with Jesus when Jairus' daughter was healed.

B It was PETER who saw Moses and Elijah on the mountain-top speaking to Jesus.

A But it was also PETER, warming his hands at the fireside, who denied that he knew Jesus.

Three times he said that he didn't know Jesus.

B And by the lakeside, Jesus took him to one side and three times asked if he loved him. PETER was restored to being a faithful follower and friend once again.

A Jesus returned to heaven to be with God his father on the day we call Ascension day.

B Before he left them, Jesus promised his friends that, after he returned to heaven, they would receive the Holy Spirit. At Pentecost the Spirit came as fire and wind. The frightened followers became people of great courage and purpose.

A It was PETER who spoke in Jerusalem when three thousand people became new followers. They were the first members of what is today the worldwide Christian church.

B God showed PETER that the message of Jesus was for everyone—not just those who followed the Jewish religion.

A PETER was a faithful fisherman, follower and friend.

Sing: 'Fisherman, follower and friend'

★ ★ ★ ★ ★ **PRAYER** ★ ★ ★ ★ ★

Father God, thank you for all those who have loved you down the ages. Help us to follow in their footsteps. Amen

Reproduced with permission from *Year-round assemblies* published by BRF 2003 (1 84101 328 5)

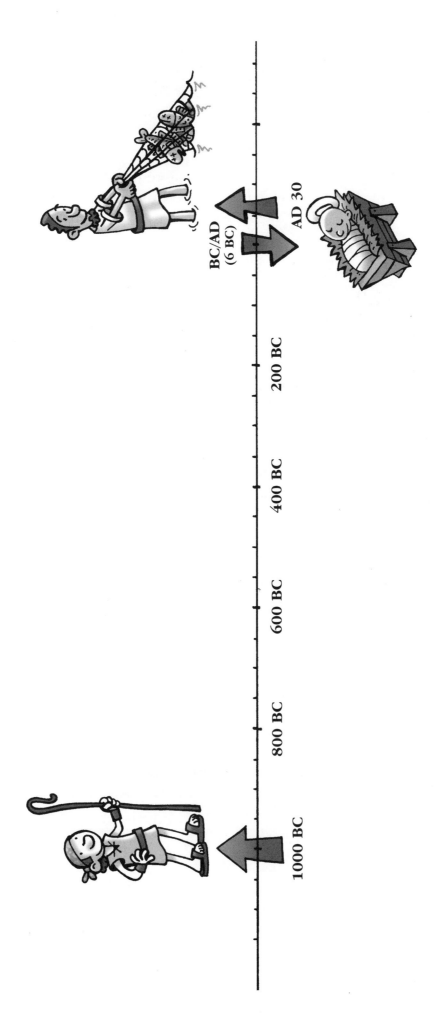

Extension Material

HYMNS

The suggested songs are the three theme songs for each term. These can be incorporated into the assembly at the appropriate place.

PSHCE LINKS

Key Stage 1
1b, 2a, 2b, 4a, 4b, 4c

Key Stage 2
1a, 2a, 2e, 4a, 4b, 4c, 4f

SUGGESTED ACTIVITIES

 Discuss the various characteristics of the three people that the assemblies have focused on. What do they all have in common? How do they differ?

 Discuss how the characters all have similar attributes, even though they lived hundreds of years apart. How do those attributes still manifest themselves today in our society, even though we are living hundreds of years after Peter died? What do you predict we might find in hundreds of years from now?

 Write an account of your opinion of the Bible characters, with a view to burying it for someone to find many years from now. How will you support your opinions?

 Write a chronological report of the three characters, summing up the main events in their lives. What will you choose to put in your report and what will you leave out?

 Choose a scene from any of the assemblies and, with a group, work out a 'freeze frame' of the event. How will you make it easy for other people to know what you are trying to show?

 Act out a modern-day scene using Peter as the main character. How might he talk, react and look if he were alive today?

 Carry out some further research either about one of the main characters, or about another character mentioned in the stories. What can you conclude from your findings about this person? Where did you go to do your research?

VISUAL AIDS REQUIRED

Interactive cards or OHP acetates are used in assemblies where the whole audience has a part to play. It is suggested that the response is either printed in large letters on a card or shown on an overhead projector. Some assemblies have further incidental OHP visuals to support the story.

AUTUMN TERM

1 World map showing Israel (p. 16)
   Time-line showing David, Jesus and the year 2000 (p. 17)

2 Interactive cards/OHP
   David and Goliath (p. 22)

6 Interactive cards/OHP
   David and his army enter Jerusalem (p. 39)
   The ark of the covenant (p. 40)
   The Ten Commandments (p. 41)

8 David's titles: cards/OHP
   David the shepherd boy (p. 50)
   David the musician (p. 51)
   David the king (p. 52)
   David the man who loved God (p. 53)

9 Names with 'son': cards/OHP

SPRING TERM

12 John the Baptist (p. 74)

13 Interactive cards/OHP
    Names of disciples on cards/OHP

15 Scroll

16 Interactive cards/OHP
    The farmer (p. 91)

18 Passover: bowl of salt water, bitter herbs, charosheth paste, four cups of wine
    Chalice and paten (if available)
    'His love never fails': card/OHP
    Chalice and paten picture (p. 100)

20 Interactive cards/OHP

SUMMER TERM

21 Interactive cards/OHP
    Map

23 The transfiguration (p. 126)

26 Interactive cards/OHP

28 White sheet with animal outline cut-outs
    Peter's dream (p. 148)

30 Interactive cards/OHP
    Time-line showing David, Jesus and Peter (p. 158)
    Children's paintings